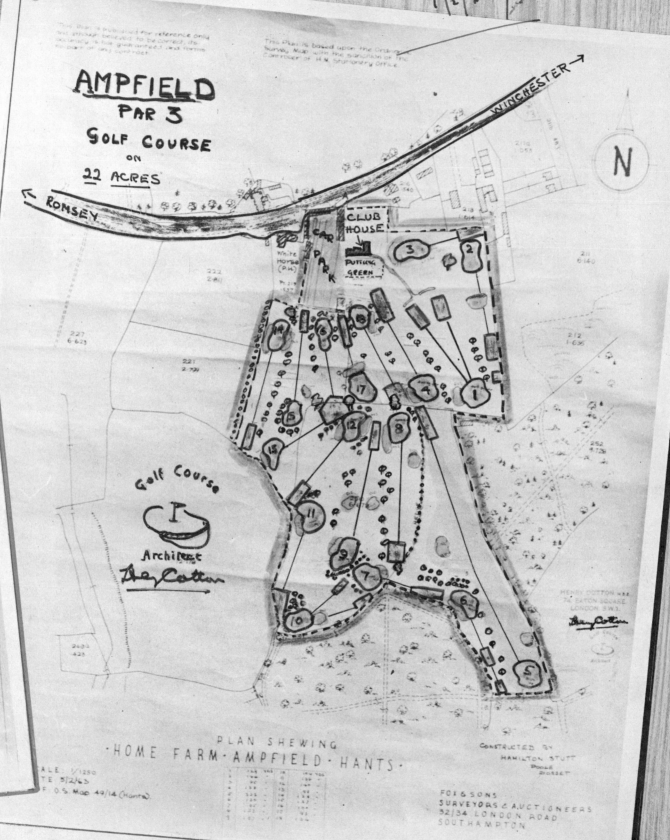

HERD from NNW
9/2/66.

AMPFIELD
PAR 3
GOLF COURSE
ON
22 ACRES

WINCHESTER →

← ROMSEY

N

CLUB HOUSE

CAR PARK

PUTTING GREEN

White Horse (P.H.)

Golf Course

Architect

PLAN SHEWING
HOME FARM · AMPFIELD · HANTS ·

CONSTRUCTED BY
HAMILTON STUTT
POOLE
DORSET

FOX & SONS
SURVEYORS & AUCTIONEERS
32/34 LONDON ROAD
SOUTHAMPTON

SCALE: 1/1250
DATE 5/2/63
F. O.S. Map 49/14 (Hants)

The
Picture Story
of the Golf Game
by Henry Cotton

Some of the photographs in this book have been supplied by kind courtesy of
ACTION PHOTOS
G M COWIE
SPORT AND GENERAL PRESS
AGENCY LIMITED
TOPICAL PRESS AGENCY
IAN JOY

Cover Design by World Distributors (Manchester) Ltd
Book Layout by Artes Graphicae Ltd, London

Published by World Distributors (Manchester) Ltd
36 Great Russell Street, London WC1

Printed and bound in England by
Jarrold and Sons Ltd, Norwich

Contents

The Game and I	8
The first putt	12
With ball and club	15
Clubs, competitions and courses	22
Rules: then and now	27
Dressed for golf	29
The incomparable caddie	35
The Amateurs and their game	39
The Walker Cup	49
The beginning of the Open	53
The Open between the wars	59
The Open after the Second World War	72
The Ryder Cup	88
The Tournament scene	94
Ladies of the links	103
The Curtis Cup	111
Golfing around the world	113
Short courses and driving range	126
Kings of the courses	130
Golf's future hopes	142
All the world plays golf	146
Anything can happen in golf	153

The Game and I

Golf has been a way of life to me for as long as I can remember. Besides playing and teaching the game I have constructed golf clubs and courses and tested various forms of golfing attire for comfort and practicality. My contribution to the history of the game has been exhilarating, every moment and every aspect of it. My enthusiasm continues unabated; indeed, I cannot imagine a time or situation in which I would have lost interest in this Royal and Ancient game.

Heredity may have played some part in shaping my career, for my father was a keen player. He encouraged my brother, Leslie, and me to play as soon as we could stand upright. A golf net was built in the garage adjoining our home and we spent all our free hours, night and day, pounding balls into it.

On leaving school Leslie became assistant to George Oke at Fulwell and at the age of sixteen, after passing my Matriculation Certificate, I turned professional and joined him as junior boy of all work. Daily, for hours at a time, I sandpapered clubheads and shafts for twelve shillings and sixpence a week, and though this was a dreary task it did much to strengthen my wrists and fingers. All my spare moments were spent in practice, but I was rarely asked to play with a member, being the youngest and least important of the assistants. After a few months I got a job as assistant at Rye; and I got plenty of practice on this grand course. I missed no chance to swing a club, making opportunities as I went along: on a dawn errand to fetch milk from a farm I would make my way across the course, hitting a ball as I went.

In 1926, when I was just nineteen years old, I began my first full professional appointment at Langley Park, Kent, and winning the Kent Professional Championship five years in succession really gave impetus to my golfing ambitions.

As a member of the Professional Golfers' Association I was eligible for all tournaments, although there were not many in those days. I had some successes, one being to finish runner-up in the *News of the World* Match Play Championship in 1928, an event I was later to win three times and in which I was twice more an unsuccessful finalist.

But my goal was to win the Open Championship. With this in mind I decided to plunge my small savings on a trip to America to study American playing methods. I received a wonderful spartan training there with a hard-working bunch who had to win to eat, and it was then that I discovered how to play from 'inside to out': hooking the ball in from the right.

Meanwhile I kept pegging away at the object of my golfing desires: 'The Open'; leading at one stage and finishing only three shots out at St. Andrews in 1933.

It was a dream come true when I won my first Open title at Royal St. George's, Sandwich, in 1934. I could see my end of the rainbow when I did 67 and 65 to lead by

I prefer to change in my car and often eat there between rounds, as this enables me to keep to my diet and get my feet up and relax, without wasting energy in useless chatter.

seven shots at the halfway stage; but my greatest triumph was in overcoming a most violent attack of stomach cramp in the final round to win by five shots. It is also satisfying to reflect that my 65 is still the lowest score of the Open, and to have achieved a 67 and a qualifying round of 66 all in the one week on that great course was one of the highlights of my career.

I won again at Carnoustie in 1937, when the Press slipped off their duckboards in their waterlogged tent. It was on the final day and there was danger of play being abandoned. My final 71 was one of the best rounds of my life – it was only one over the course record – and I will always remember the last hole, where I needed a four for the 70. With two burns to cross this was a tense moment, but I did not play safe but hit hard and landed in the hole-high bunker. I played out of the hard wet sand and, with two putts, got down in five to win by two strokes.

Then came the Second World War, followed by a long period of ill-health which caused my discharge from the R.A.F. and ended in a serious abdominal operation with a year's convalescence, when I was not allowed to hit a shot. This seriously affected my play in the first post-war championship at St. Andrews in 1946.

After a trip to America and plenty of good food my health improved and I won my last Open title by five shots at Muirfield in 1948, on a great course of narrow fairways with plenty of rough. Before setting out on my second round I was introduced to His Majesty, King George. I scored a 66, and this 'Royal' round was the crown of my golfing success.

Golf has given me much pleasure. I hope I can transmit some of this enjoyment to readers of this book.

Henry Cotton

A Ryder Cup team Back row (*left to right*): Commander R. T. C. Roe (Manager), *Jimmy Adams, Max Faulkner, Eric Green, Charles Ward, Reg Horne.* Sitting (*left to right*): *Sam King, Fred Daly, Henry Cotton, Dai Rees, Arthur Lees.*

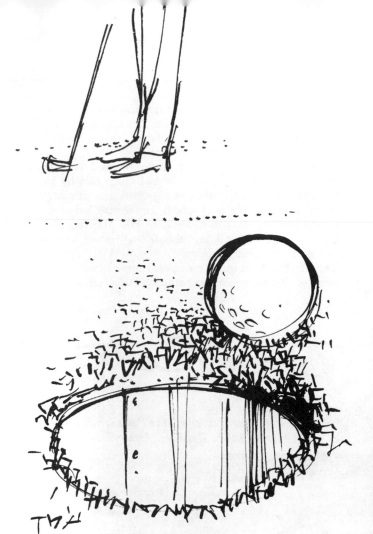

The first putt

The glory of originating the Royal game of golf is claimed by many countries and each claimant has its enthusiastic supporters. Its parentage has been credited to the Dutch, the Irish, and the Scots, and even the invading Roman soldiers are enthusiastically hailed by some as its inventors. In keeping with the tradition of mighty conquerors, of course, they are alleged to have used stones as balls.

In outlining the theoretical origins of the game I do not propose to enter the contending ranks. There is no conclusive proof of either the place or time of the game's beginnings. Perhaps Adam and Eve enjoyed a quiet round with an apple, though if they had we might all be golfers in Eden now. I think it more likely that a shepherd on some lonely hilltop, bored with counting his sheep, began idly to strike a pebble with his crook and accidentally knocked it into a rabbit hole. Then, having nothing better to do anyway, he probably tried to repeat the performance.

The Claimants. The theory that the present game of golf evolved from the Dutch game of *het kolven* is based mainly on the similarity of the clubs used in both games. But a much larger ball, weighing nearly two pounds, was used in kolven.

Dating back to the fifteenth century, kolven was sometimes played through the streets of Dutch towns, which must have presented a considerable hazard to any slow-moving citizens. The protection of these unfortunates probably resulted in the edict issued in 1398 by Albert, Duke of Bavaria, conferring on the citizens of Brielle the right to play kolven outside the ramparts of the town. The game was also played inside churches. It is hard today to visualise this peculiar setting, but in the Middle Ages the body of a church was kept clear of seats and the congregation stood round the sides during worship. It seems hardly conceivable that the game we know as golf could have been born within such restricted boundaries. Some very attractive Dutch paintings of the seventeenth century depict kolven being played on ice. The ball would have run fantastic distances in these conditions and here could have been no finesse or short shots to a target.

Kolven is still played in some parts of Holland, but it bears little resemblance to golf.

The Irish claim to golfing parentage was established by the inclusion of the game in the curriculum of the revived Irish Olympic Games. Irish theorists held that golf evolved from the older Celtic game of hurley or shunty.

The Illegal Game. It is, however, almost universally accepted that the Scots devised the essential features of our present game. The first official mention of golf in Scotland coupled it with football in the famous 1457 Act of Parliament which ordered that these two games 'be utterly cryit dune and not to be used'. This was in the reign of James II of Scotland and golf had become so popular by then that men were neglecting archery

Roman soldiers are depicted hitting stones with wooden clubs, in a game devised to while away some idle hours as they guarded their forts.

While their flock grazed peacefully near by, shepherds in ancient times may have passed many a pleasant afternoon in their own version of a round of golf.

practice at a time when there was always danger of attack from England. While these hostilities lasted the playing of golf was illegal in Scotland: forbidden in successive decrees by James III and by James IV in 1491. When a treaty of peace was finally negotiated between the two countries the event was celebrated in a manner acclaimed by enthusiasts as highly appropriate. On 22 February 1502, the day the treaty was ratified, James IV played his celebrated match with the Earl of Bothwell.

So with peace came golf again; not only to Scotland, but also to England as a result of the friendlier atmosphere now prevailing between these neighbouring nations. Soon golf links began to encircle the coasts of Britain, finding ideal settings in areas of heathland where poor soil discouraged cultivation.

The 'Royal' Game. Before long the game began to assume its 'Royal' connotation. During nearly two hundred years, from 1502 until 1688, every reigning monarch of the Stuart line, two Kings and one Queen of Scotland and four Kings of the United Kingdom, was a golfer.

When Scotland's James VI became James I of England he took his favourite clubs with him to his new throne. He also introduced his two young sons to the game, which they probably played in London's Royal Park.

As a young man one of these sons, later to become James II, was challenged by two English noblemen to play them in a foursome with a Scottish partner of his own choice.

He selected a shoemaker named John Patersone, and this improbable pair won the first international match with ease. A large sum of money had been wagered on the result and the future king handed half the winnings to Patersone, who used the money to buy himself a house in Edinburgh.

The house still stands and on one of its walls can be seen the family coat-of-arms which the Prince bestowed on Patersone to commemorate their victory, surmounted by a crest depicting a dexter hand grasping a golf club with the motto 'Far and Sure'.

But although they had fostered the game, not all the Scots wholeheartedly approved of golf. The Presbyterians, being of strict religious principles, were rather dubious about the sport and, in 1604, Robert Robinson of Perth was made to sit in the 'seat of repentance' for playing golf on Sunday.

Her love of golf also contributed to the downfall of Mary Queen of Scots. One of the charges brought against the beautiful and ill-fated Mary at her trial was that, within a few days of the murder of her husband Darnley, she had been seen 'playing golf'.

But if it penalised, golf also had its compensations. The last historical golfing anecdote of the Scottish Royal line relates how Bonnie Prince Charlie relieved the boredom of his Italian exile by knocking a ball about in the Borghese gardens.

Soldiers enjoying a game of golf as it was played in its infancy. In the background is a castle, where the soldiers were presumably stationed

With the same castle in the background we see a soldier arrested for neglecting archery practice in favour of golf.

With ball and club

Golfing equipment may be elaborate, specially designed or mass-produced, but the basic essentials are the same today as they were at the game's inception: a ball and a club.

As golfers enthuse over the brilliant execution of a difficult stroke or the winning of a closely contested match, so they also find intense interest in the study of the wooden and iron clubs from the benches and forges of the great handcraftsmen of the past and in the balls, featheries and 'gutta various' of former years. The development of golfing equipment is an essential part of the history of the game.

The earliest golf balls were probably made of turned boxwood. This theory is supported by a dispatch written during the reign of James I, which describes the siege of a castle during which the cannon balls burst into fragments 'like golf balls'. This description rules out any thought of feather-filled balls being used at this time.

A Fine Art. With the invention of the 'featheries' ball-making became one of the fine arts, for feather balls were constructed at great trouble to the maker and at a corresponding expense to the players. In making the ball, four sections of leather were first stitched together, leaving one small hole. The leather was then reversed so that the seams were on the inside. Feathers were then pushed in through the hole by means of an iron spike fixed in a wooden framework upon which the ballmaker had to lean all his weight. It is most unlikely that this man was fit, or even keen, to have a round of golf after such herculean efforts. However his labours cost the golfer the then astronomical sum of two shillings and sixpence a ball, and balls could cost as much as four or five shillings each.

Feather balls could be driven for considerable distances. History has it that a player named John Gibson made a series of measured drives on Glasgow Green ranging from 175 yards to 222 yards and balls could hardly run far on the uncut turf of those days. But their high cost and their tendency to become waterlogged outweighed their merits.

There is no record of the originator of the idea of using gutta-percha for golf balls, but the gutta ball first appeared in 1848. It soon replaced the leather featherie, as they wore longer and they also flew much better when their smooth surfaces had been dented by the iron clubs. When this fact was noted it was decided to mark the balls artificially with a chisel-headed hammer and these hand-hammered balls were used up to 1880 when moulds superseded the hammering process.

As a result of the guttas economy in comparison with the short-lived and expensive feathery balls they became the means of attracting a whole new contingent of players to the game. Their price was reasonable at twelve shillings a dozen, but an obvious disadvantage was their weight, which made it hard work for a player to get the ball up in the air.

Feathers and a feather ball. The top hat contains the exact quantity of feathers
which had to be stuffed into the specially sewn skin. It was a feat of skill, patience, and indeed sheer strength.
In wet conditions the varnished skin soon got soggy.

An early golfing hero, Allan Robertson was a St. Andrews man, born in 1815. He stands with his 'tools', one a very long-headed wooden club with a spliced head. Older golfers claimed that Allan's swing was perfection.
A maker of feather balls, he bought up all the gutta balls he could find in an attempt to preserve his industry by preventing the spread of the gutta. His valiant, though perhaps misguided, attempt failed and he died in 1858, two years before the creation of the Open Championship.

America's Contribution. America's first and most important contribution to golf was in the development of the rubber-cored ball, which was invented by a Cleveland golfer named Coburn Haskell and which revolutionised the game. The Haskell ball had a covering of gutta-percha enclosing a ball of rubber thread wound under tension round a solid rubber core. Gone was the fearful effort of getting the solid gutta ball into the air: this new ball was lively and the skilled player did wonders with it. The cost at first was rather prohibitive at thirty shillings each, but the price was later stabilised at two shillings and sixpence.

The ball achieved its first success when Walter Travis won the American Amateur Championship with it in 1901. When it came to England, Sandy Herd, using it for the first time, won the Open Championship at Hoylake in 1902, defeating Harry Vardon, who was using the old gutta, by one stroke.

The Haskell ball was very responsive, easy to lift well into the air from a tee and to raise from off the ground through the green, and a real flyer off an iron club. Experimenters over the years reduced the size and increased the weight of the ball so that it was capable of being driven over ever-increasing distances. To restrict the distance to which a ball could be hit the Royal and Ancient in 1920 imposed a minimum limit of size of 1·62 inches and a maximum limit of weight of 1·62 ounces. This restriction came into force in May 1921.

The rubber-cored ball we use today is substantially the same as the original Haskell; the cover thickness and tension of winding have been increased and the solid core replaced by a liquid centre. This liquid centre varies with the individual maker, but I have heard of

Giant Archie Compston in real jungle country in the days of the hickory shafts. Notice the broad-soled niblick, one of the first of this type.
A successor to this early model is to be found in every player's bag today.

Hugh Philip, the maker of the first fine, well-balanced club. A Hugh Philip club was to a golfer what a Stradivarius is to a violinist and clubs made by this great craftsman were much in demand.
But as the game grew in popularity and the demand exceeded the supply, firms specialising in the manufacture of clubs developed.

honey and boiled tapioca and also of jam being used. All these modifications have one aim in view: to make the ball go further.

The British ball is smaller and supposed to bore better into a head or crosswind than the American one, but our friends from across the Atlantic use their own over here in any weather . . . and they frequently win. Perhaps for this reason general feeling is veering towards the bigger American ball, which is the same weight as ours but 1·68 inches in diameter. British manufacturers have been speeding up its production and no doubt we shall all be using it soon. I feel we must if we are to rival America again.

Development of Clubs. Golf clubs were made by the bow-maker in the days when archery was still used in warfare. Unfortunately no specimens of these craftsmen's art have been preserved. A clubhouse in Troon boasts of the clubs accredited with being the oldest in existence. They are a set of eight which were discovered many years ago in a boarded-up house in Hull, along with a newspaper bearing the date 1741. The clubs are believed to have been already old when they were placed in the cupboard and probably belonged to the period of the Stuart kings. These clubs are crudely finished, as could be expected, but the most amazing thing about them is their size. They are gargantuan instruments, so long in the shaft that it is difficult to understand how our golfing heroes of old managed to hit a little ball into a small hole with such a weapon.

The earliest iron clubs, from the clumsy 'Carrick' irons which are included in so many collections of old clubs, were excessively deep in the blade. It was only the advent of the guttie which made many realise that these new balls were admirably adapted to the use of iron clubs in the approach shots. The development of the iron clubs was carried a step further by the use of the niblick for the shorter pitch shots and this eventually led to the invention of the mashie, the equivalent of the No. 5 iron.

The Americans developed the use of lofted clubs for the shorter pitch shots, using the loft of the club not to toss the ball higher in the air, but to hit down on the ball,

One of the earliest firms to specialise in golf equipment was Gibsons of Kinghorn, Scotland. This firm made the first British autographed clubs, bearing the name of James Braid, about 1907. Here is a group of workers at the factory, some in the front row proudly holding the hickory shafts they are making. Those in the white aprons were the wood workers; the others were the hand forgers of iron heads. These workers beat the iron heads out of short iron bars. Their job was dirty and hot, but very skilled. Scotland was once the exclusive producer of fine golf clubs. Now America produces millions of top quality clubs every year, but Scotland still makes the world's finest golf clubs.

Douglas Rolland and Sandy Herd in the days of the gutta ball and the long pear-shaped spliced drivers with rough thick leather grips. Rolland was the Harry Weetman of his day, hitting the gutta long distances and this ball really did need ferocious attacking to get it away. It was claimed that two hundred and fifty yards was the maximum distance a gutta could be driven in the most favourable conditions and usually the best players drove only around one hundred and eighty to one hundred and ninety yards.

1 An early centre-shafted club. 2 Also illegal is this club for playing from sand. The sand was intended to go through the hole, thus reducing resistance to the swing. 3 Another putter which is now illegal. This has a reflector that the player could line up with the flagstick. 4 A hammer-headed putter, obviously the perfect putting club, but now illegal under the ruling that the clubface must be wider in the face than the distance from front to back.

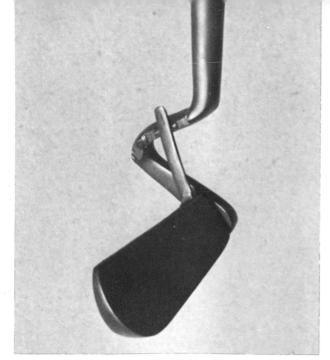

The first adjustable iron, now displayed in the Museum of Golf in the clubhouse of the Royal and Ancient Club. Various lofts can be put on this club by springing the lever into different notches. Such clubs are illegal in tournament golf, but modern editions are still sold for those playing golf without caddies and not wishing to carry any other clubs.

Champion Sam Snead with his famous old driver. This club head had four new steel shafts in it over fifteen years before the head finally cracked irreparably. He has never found a driver to replace it.

with the hands in advance of the club head. This produced a low-flying ball with a tremendous amount of back spin in the much discussed 'wedge shot'.

Another development that helped to simplify the mechanics of the game was the substitution of steel shafts for hickory. The steel shaft enabled sets to be matched, so that the whole range of clubs, numbers 1 to 4 woods, numbers 1 to 9 irons, and even the putter, could be expertly graduated in length and weight, loft and degree of whippiness to fit with one another. Today if a player has a favourite club which suits his play, clubmakers can use this as a model and make him a whole set to suit his individual swing.

Nowadays there is a special club for every conceivable stroke, a development which our forefathers may regard with scorn from their golfing heaven. The contention that scientific standardisation has destroyed the individuality in clubs cannot be argued. Old-time golfers were given to naming their clubs, one famous lawyer having a niblick called 'Faith' because, as he liked to tell his friends, faith can move mountains. Nowadays the only club whose choice allows scope for individual fancy is the putter and probably the most famous weapon the game has ever known belonged to one of the greatest ever golfers, if not *the* greatest: it was Bobby Jones' own putter, 'Calamity Jane'.

For the golfer who has everything: real mink club head covers. Obviously an American luxury; where else could they have originated?

21

Clubs
competitions and
courses

Early golf courses were wholly natural: rabbits and sheep were the only greenkeepers, and no boundaries separated the course from Farmer Brown's sheep or prevented its use as a playground by any neighbouring children. On these first crude courses all distinctions of rank were levelled in the enjoyment of the game, as the lords of the land swung clubs with the artisans and peasants.

The middle of the eighteenth century saw the formation of the first golf clubs and, with them, the beginning of the modern history of golf. The first step in the formation of almost every club was the presentation of a trophy for competition: the instituting of competitions went hand-in-hand with the growth of clubs.

As golf was introduced into England by the Scots no one can dispute that the oldest clubs began north of the border.

The First Golf Club. The links of Leith were much frequented in the beginning of the seventeenth century, and some of the players came to be known as the 'Gentlemen Golfers of Edinburgh'. In 1744 several of these gentlemen petitioned the city of Edinburgh for a Silver Club for yearly competition at Leith. The Trophy was given and the competition was declared open to as many 'Noblemen, Gentlemen or other golfers of Great Britain or Ireland as should send in their entries during the eight days preceding the competition'. The winner was to be called the 'Captain of the Golf'; in modern terms 'the Champion Golfer'.

But this first competition caused hardly a ripple in the golfing world. No one crossed the sea or travelled far to compete, so that it became a purely local contest won by John Rattray, an Edinburgh surgeon, who repeated his success the following year.

This became an annual local event for twenty years, with no outside invasion, and in 1764 the 'Captains of the Golf', the winners of the trophy, petitioned the City of Edinburgh for authority 'to admit such Noblemen and Gentlemen as they approve to be members of the Company of Golfers and to restrict the competition for the Silver Club to these members'. Permission being given, the Honourable Company of Edinburgh Golfers, whose headquarters are now at Muirfield, was established. If we take the date of their first competition in 1744 as being the date of the formation of the club, this makes it the first official golf club.

History shows that James I established Blackheath as a golfing venue as early as 1608, playing over and round the rabbit warrens. But the Blackheath Golf Club, the first established club in England, was not formed until 1766, when a trophy was presented for competition among the local players. This silver driver, now a treasured heirloom in the present clubhouse at Eltham, bears the inscription 'August 16, 1766. The gift of Mr. Henry Foot to the Honourable Company of Golfers at Blackheath'.

St. Andrews Begins. The example of the Leith golfers was followed by the St. Andrews men in 1754. Twenty two 'noblemen and gentlemen, being admirers of the ancient and healthful exercise of the Golf' formed a club at St. Andrews, the best natural links in Scotland, when they provided money for a silver club to be played for in open competition. Baillie William Landale won against the not very considerable opposition of three other entrants.

Every winner was expected to affix a silver or gold piece, in the form of a golf ball, to the trophy, rather a similar idea to the President's putter being laden with another golf ball after every annual competition at Rye. As it was the practice to make this silver ball as close a replica of the winner's ball as possible some of the older trophies realistically mark the progress of ball-making during the past two hundred years.

The original trophy of the Royal and Ancient dates from 1754 and it carried on valiantly until 1819, by which time it was close packed with balls attached by successive captains. This club must surely have had a longer shaft, for history relates that it found room for silver balls until 1922, when the Duke of Windsor, then Prince of Wales,

became captain of the club and presented another duplicate of the original club on which to hang the yearly mementoes. There are now three silver clubs at St. Andrews.

All the precious trophies of the Royal and Ancient are for scratch competitions. The Gold Medals, one presented by King William IV and the other presented by the club in 1806, are the first and second prizes of the autumn meeting. The Silver Cross and Silver Medal are the first and second prizes at the spring meeting, while the George Glennie Medal presented by the Royal Blackheath Club is for the best scratch aggregate over the two meetings. These are all Challenge Trophies to be held for one year. The club was known as The St. Andrews Club until 1834 when William IV became its patron and agreed that it be called 'The Royal and Ancient Golf Club of St. Andrews'.

Captains Royal. The captain of the club is elected annually. At the autumn meeting the captain-elect plays himself in by driving a ball from the first tee in the early

A typical sports pavilion of the early days of golf. Holding the club is the famous professional Tom Williamson who stayed with his club at Hollinwell, Notts, for over fifty years. Many groups would be well advised to content themselves with modest accommodation like this when founding a club, rather than burden their finances with an elaborate clubhouse and correspondingly extravagant upkeep charges.

CLUBHOUSE   BULWELL FOREST 1900

morning. As the only player in the competition he emerges winner and simultaneously captain, and so the old tradition is preserved. During their year of office captains travel all over the country speaking at dinners, at which they wear their red tailcoats.

There have been several Royal captains: Edward VII in 1863; Prince Leopold in 1876; the Duke of Windsor when he was Prince of Wales in 1922; King George VI in 1930 when he was Duke of York, and the Duke of Kent in 1937. The Royal and Ancient is the governing golf club of the world: it frames the rules and its decisions are accepted by clubs throughout the world, usually now after joint discussion with the United States Golf Association for it is hoped to have an identical set of rules on both sides of the Atlantic.

In the very early days golf usually consisted of seven holes, though Leith and Blackheath, golfing pioneers of Scotland and England, began with only five holes. When Leith extended the course to seven, Blackheath followed suit, but the glory of originating the eighteen-hole course, now adopted the world over, belongs to St. Andrews.

During the fifty years following the formation of the first clubs, Leith was the most important links in Scotland. Continuous use and no greenkeeping resulted in the gradual deterioration of the course and its position

Unchanged for over a hundred years, but with back tees now, is the famous Old course at St. Andrews. It is just getting out of date for modern golf. Today spectators at Championships follow big golf from behind a rope fence, not in the manner of the crowd in this photograph.

of eminence was taken by St. Andrews. There were then twelve holes along the shore, and the golfers played eleven straight out to the far end of the course and then turned round and played them back again, finishing the round by holing out near the first tee. Today a number of St. Andrews' gigantic greens are used for both outgoing and incoming holes, proving the soundness of the original idea. Prestwick, the first Open Championship course, also had twelve holes, but they were played in a circle just as many courses are now laid out in two loops, returning to the clubhouse at the 9th and 18th holes. The stalwarts of Prestwich often played three rounds a day, making thirty six holes.

In 1764 the Royal and Ancient decided, probably on the advice of some golf architects on their committee, to convert the first four holes into two so that out and home made a round of eighteen holes. Their decision fashioned the standard golf courses of the world.

There are now four courses at St. Andrews: The Old, which is the course where the Championships are decided; The New; The Jubilee and The Eden.

The Old Course is different from any other course and is sometimes an acquired taste with newcomers. The great Bobby Jones called it a cow patch after his first time round. Later he acclaimed it the greatest golf course of them all and said it was the spot he would choose to live if he were obliged to live on a golf course.

There are seven tremendous double greens some hundred yards wide on this course today, with two holes on each green and some awesome bunkers with centuries-old names. The Beardies, Hell, Strath, and the Principal's Nose are golfing household words. Most famous of all holes is the 17th at St. Andrews, the Road Hole, with its narrow ribbon of a green and the dreaded road just beyond and below the putting surface.

Around British Courses. Carnoustie is another great Scottish course. The Barrie Burn, a steep-sided hazard, winds about through the fairways and provides tremendous carries for the bravest players. In company with some great golfers, including Ben Hogan and Tommy Armour, I am proud to have won a Championship here and so become part of golfing history.

The great Championship course of Muirfield, on the edge of the Firth of Forth, is the home of the Honourable Company of Edinburgh Golfers. The clubhouse has a magnificent view over the course to the Forth. The Open, The Amateur, and The Scottish Championships take their regular turn here. Walter Hagen had his name engraved on the Championship Cup in 1929; I won there in 1948 and South African Gary Player won The Open the last time it was played there, in 1959.

Of the great English courses Royal Birkdale is now an automatic favourite for big events.

Its advantages include adequate parking facilities and space for a 'Tent Town'. Three Open Championships have been held on this rugged course with its tall sand dunes and tough willow scrub which traps any ball which is the least bit off the line. The 1965 Open and Ryder Cup matches have been played there on a redesigned and extended course.

Royal Lytham and St. Anne's has a long and distinguished list of events held over the sandy course, with its great carries, strategic bunkers and cruel rough. Its most famous hole is the dog's-leg 17th where the greatest of all American amateurs, Bobby Jones, won the first of his Open Championships in 1926. His winning shot at the 17th was so wonderful and noteworthy that it is commemorated by a brass plaque embedded in the side of the bunker. A lady visitor to the spot many years later was much impressed by this and asked in awed tones, 'Is it true that Bobby Jones is buried here?'

The course of the Royal Liverpool Golf Club at Hoylake in Cheshire is rich in golfing history. Here the first Walker Cup match with America was played and many Open and Amateur Championships have been held here since. Courses tend to get progressively longer nowadays, but Hoylake was the first which measured over seven thousand yards. It is a flat course, but with out-of-bounds limits everywhere it is a big test of nerves.

The south of England abounds in beautiful golfing country. One of the greatest of all inland courses is Walton Heath, which has been host to the English Amateur Championship and is the home course of the *News of the World* Matchplay Championship. It contains two beautiful, heather-girt courses and has one of the finest and most luxurious clubhouses in the country.

Other two-course clubs are Wentworth, scene of the Ryder and Canada Cup matches and many professional tournaments, neighbouring Sunningdale and the Berkshire Club on the road to Ascot. There are many other fine clubs in the Home Counties, which boast of two hundred and fifty clubs around London.

The courses of Sandwich, Princes and Royal St. George have seen many stirring battles and any mention of golf in Wales includes the clubs of Royal Porthcawl and Harlech.

The courses of northern and southern Ireland equal each other in grandeur. The Open and Amateur Championships have been played at Royal Portrush and the Amateur and Canada Cup have been held at Portmarnock, one of my favourite seaside tests.

The Ladies' British Championship has wandered over Ireland to Royal Portrush, Portmarnock and Royal County Down, where it was again played in 1963 after an interval of thirty six years.

Honoured by Royalty. There are seventy-one Royal golf courses in the world, the designation being conferred by the reigning monarch or a member of the Royal family, usually through patronage or playing on the course.

In Belgium there are four Royal courses, an honour conferred on them by the King of the Belgians. The

Belgian Royal family have supported and played golf for many years, and both ex-King Leopold and King Baudouin have single figure handicaps.

All the other Royal courses stem from our own Royal family.

Courses are situated in all sorts of soil and they lie in all kinds of beautiful settings.

There are still hundreds of courses which are now out of date. Courses which were built forty years ago when the equipment was comparatively inferior are often not adequate tests for players today. But gradually these courses are being modernised and there are no bad courses being built today, for the game now possesses dozens of qualified architects, and amateur course builders can call on a vast fund of data which has collected over the golfing years.

The links of the Honourable Company of Edinburgh Golfers at Muirfield: present home of the world's oldest Golf Club. This is a photograph of the 13th green, with the Firth of Forth in the distance.

Rules
then and now

The game of golf started as an agreeable pastime with its conditions of play controlled by gentlemen's honour. There was no need for formal rules; disputed points were referred to the amiable decision of one or two of the senior players. It was inevitable that these decisions varied from place to place, and even the most sporting of early British golfers must occasionally have jibed at some of the odd rulings under such a system. But golf was still a game in the strict sense of the word: to be played, enjoyed and then forgotten.

This attitude was changed by the introduction of competitions: though the game was no less friendly and enjoyable, the result now began to assume an importance of its own. It became necessary to establish common rules. When twenty two Noblemen and Gentlemen of St. Andrews met on 14 May, 1754, to compete for a Silver Club, they played to the first set of thirteen rules for matchplay competitions, impressively entitled 'Articles and laws in playing the golf'.

The most interesting of these rules was the one which decreed that golfers must tee their ball within club-length of the hole. This suggests a stark contrast with present-day putting greens. Another ruling, that if a ball were stopped by a man, horse or dog it had to be played where it lay, presents an amusing picture of the traffic interruptions our golfing forefathers had to endure.

As conditions improved the ball was teed farther from the hole and, in 1851, St. Andrews made a further effort to preserve the putting surface, increasing the distance to four feet.

For more than one hundred years match play was the accepted form of golf and these original rules sufficed. But as stroke play competitions gained in popularity and as the number of contestants increased, a more rigorous code was needed. The Aberdeen code of 1783 tried to provide this and did, indeed, introduce a number of drastic regulations. One of them forbade the removal of 'stones, loose sand or other impediments, when putting at the hole'. A less restricting rule replaced this in 1893 which prohibited the removal of loose impediments when the ball was 'lying in or touching a hazard'. This rule still applies today when loose impediments can be lifted anywhere except when both the ball and the loose impediment lie in or touch a hazard. Another difficult condition, 'lost ball, lost hole', came into force in 1882 and was an accepted rule until 1920.

While these rules were all very well for match play, the growing number of stroke play enthusiasts still felt that a special set of rules should be designed for them.

In a game that now girdled the globe a further need was keenly felt for greater elasticity in the rules. This was especially apparent in some remote outposts of the Empire, where nature and the local animal life presented the golfer with conditions never envisaged by the Scottish legislators.

Rules for a Worldwide Game. A universal code,

where 'the perspective was to be worldwide to meet the varying conditions under which the game is now played', was laid down by the Royal and Ancient Golf Club and the United States Golf Association at their conference in 1951. The most important result of their decisions was the establishment of loss of stroke and distance as the penalty for ball out of bounds, unplayable ball and lost ball. Another major decision was the abolition of the stymie, which had been a constant source of controversy because of the unfairness of one ball lying in the path of another and sometimes making it impossible for the man who had played the better shot to the green to get his ball into the hole.

There were some mourners at the deathbed of the stymie, for to loft a ball into the hole over a stymie was one of the prettiest of shots and of supreme satisfaction to the perpetrator. The retention of the shot was advocated by many who acclaimed it 'a sporting feature of the game'. But the majority opinion won and the stymie, which had been the cause of the winning and losing of many important matches, vanished for ever on New Year's Day 1952.

During the nineteenth century the method of handicapping was bad and tended to be confusing also in inter-club competitions, as each club adopted as its scratch standard the normal performance of its best players and this standard varied considerably from club to club.

Enter Colonel Bogey. A new system of handicapping, which became known as the bogey score, was conceived in the idea of a competition in which each competitor would be invited to play a match under handicap against a hypothetical opponent playing perfect golf at each hole. This resulted in the fixing of a 'ground score':

the score that a scratch player of the day would take for each hole playing perfect golf. Bogey achieved its military standing of 'Colonel' Bogey when it was adopted by the United Services Club at Gosport and somebody jokingly remarked that all members, including Bogey, had to have military rank.

Bogey is the same as our modern standard scratch score which has now been substituted as the score which a scratch golfer is expected to equal. The par of the course, an American expression for their basic score, our standard scratch score, is the basis of all handicapping.

Team play, as in the International matches and all the other joint efforts including inter-club affrays, consists of foursomes and singles. Foursome play was originally introduced into inter-club matches for purely social reasons; having decided the match in the morning by a singles, a foursome was arranged after lunch to give everybody an easy-going game. The foursome was established as part of the competition later, and it was played before the singles when it was considered that playing the singles first might, in fact, give a one-sided score and that the result of the foursome ought to count in the aggregate score.

Americans prefer four-ball matches, where each player has the opportunity to drive at every tee, to two-ball foursomes, which they call Scotch foursomes, where two players as partners play alternate strokes at each hole. Though the situation has improved over the years, the rules of golf are still very complicated: it is said to take three years to learn them all. In fact there are few people in the world with a faultless knowledge of the rules.

James I of England who, it is said, played golf at Blackheath in 1608.

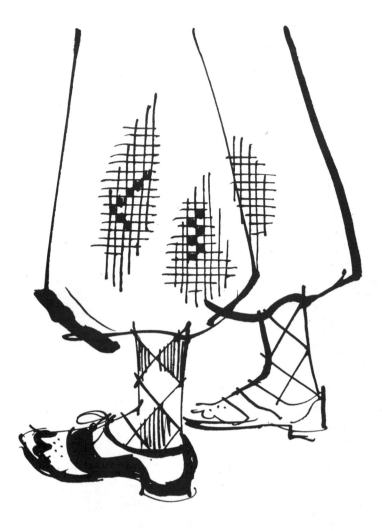

Dressed
for golf

Photographs of eighteenth-century golfers evoke feelings of sympathetic amusement and even bewilderment. Their dress was certainly in keeping with the image of a Royal game, resplendent enough for any court occasion. But however did they endure, even enjoy, a strenuous round of golf in such restricting, if splendid, clothes? It could certainly only be comfortable in fine weather.

Fashion was a serious feature of the game at this period and the choice of a uniform was regarded by clubs as a very important decision. Doublets and long hose had been worn up to the seventeen-hundreds, but now tight knee breeches, silken hose and buckled shoes were essentials in the wardrobe of the well-dressed golfer.

Red for Danger. But it was in the imaginative choice of coats and capes that golfing fashion really ran riot. Brilliant scarlet cloaks were favoured by the majority of golfers. Many writers have decried the theory that this conspicuous colour was chosen deliberately, so that golfers could easily be seen by anybody wandering on to the course who was thus warned of the danger of being struck by balls. This reason is, in fact, highly probable and red garments are still compulsory on courses over common land in many parts of the country: good sense and very attractive against the green fairways.

In 1784 the Royal and Ancient adopted a red coat with dark blue velvet cape trimmed with plain white buttons and two large buttons on each sleeve. The cape was embroidered on each side of the front with a club and ball in silver thread.

The Innerleven Golfing Society had a uniform of Prince Charles tartan. Glasgow golfers seem to have been conservative, by comparison, in plain grey. But Aberdeen had two uniforms: red jackets for play and equally resplendent blue jackets into which they changed for dining. Royal Blackheath had no separate evening attire, but they added gold epaulettes to their regulation scarlet coats for state and social occasions.

Even in literary circles one very definitely 'dressed for golf'. Pickwick designed special uniforms for members of his famous club, complete with the inevitable 'golf button'.

The wearing of a club uniform was obligatory and golfers breaking this rule were fined.

In Golfing Splendour. Nineteenth-century greens continued to be gay scenes of foppery and frippery, indeed uniforms became more and more elaborate. In 1837 members of the Burgess Golfing Society had to be equipped with 'a dress coat, colour dark claret, with black velvet collar, double-breasted and lined in the skirts with white silk or satin, prominent buttons on cuffs of coat and also on the flaps, dress vest colour primrose with smaller buttons to correspond with those on the coat'. They sported this sartorial elegance on all special occasions.

About this time too, tall hats became the mode and the means by which they were retained by their owners in

The authentic golfing attire with red coat which Royal Blackheath players once had to wear. Dai Rees presents a contrast in casual modern wear, as he holds a club of the former period in his hand.

face of strong winds remains one of golf's unsolved mysteries.

Encased in their splendidly impractical uniforms, golfers must have been badly hampered in the freedom and power of their swings, and the inevitable reaction set in during the second half of the nineteenth century when a blight of contrasting dowdiness descended upon the links. Gone was the embroidery, the velvets and satins, the brave glowing colours. The Victorian golfer set his own defiant standard in his oldest, even shabbiest suit. If a seam had given way, so much the better in this new fad for comfort and casualness which soon became a fashion. It now became possible to assess a player's merit by his golfing attire: the better the player the more disreputable and moth-eaten a jacket he felt entitled to wear.

This revolt on the links faded towards the end of the century when the Norfolk jacket and knickers came into vogue.

After the First World War came plus-fours and Fair Isle jumpers, a fashion initiated by the Duke of Windsor, then Prince of Wales. The luxurious comfort and freedom of knitwear was enthusiastically welcomed and golfers vied with one another in the startling colours of their garb. Britishers who had been mildly disapproving of the Americans' tinctorial brilliance now joined and even out-dazzled them. This progressed eventually to the University-set fashion of fishermen's jerseys and voluminous flannel bags: a case of taking comfort to an uncomfortable limit.

The refreshment staff at the 9th hole of St. Andrews in 1880. 'Drinka pinta' might have been a slogan invented by Old Tom Morris then. I find the clothes most interesting, right up to date with their drainpipe trousers.

Golf around 1880: it seems to have gone to the players' heads. In fact the fashion of the day decreed the wearing of hats, but apparently the choice of style was left to the player. The greens were very rough then, not much better than many fairways today, and the players used long-headed wooden putters. In those days a set of clubs contained more woods than irons: the opposite is the case today.

In hard collars and golfing jackets,
J. H. Taylor and Harry Vardon pause before a round
in pre-1914 days. Vardon wears knickers here, though
he later favoured plus-fours. Taylor wears trousers,
but the standard of pressing in those days
seems pretty inadequate.

The Duke of York, later King George VI, plays in Fair
Isle jumper and plus-fours, the golfing style of the
twenties. He is using a hickory-shafted driver, which
was in general use at that time.
King George, the Duke's father, also enjoyed golf and
played whenever duty permitted.

American stars of the thirties greatly influenced the dress on and off the course of top American and British
golfers for many years. In this picture are (left to right): Jimmy Hines, U.S. P.G.S. Champion; Olin Dutra, U.S. Open
Champion 1932; Billy Burke, U.S. Open Champion 1931; Walter Hagen, U.S. Open Champion 1914 and 1919, and
Al Free, a friend of the players and owner of a smart New York men's store.

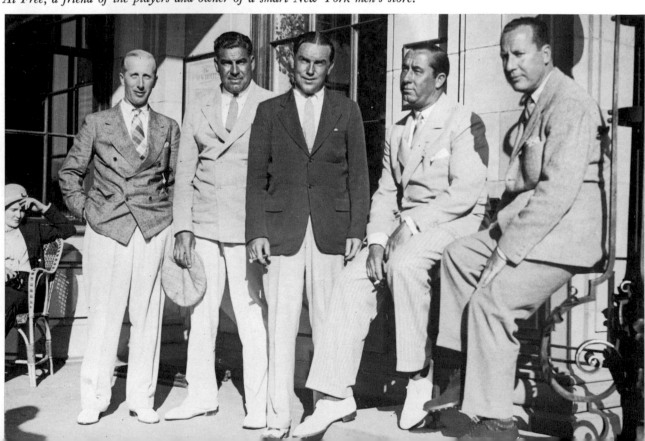

Today's golfing fashions tend towards an informal uniformity and are, perhaps for the first time, suitable. Players in dark blazers off the course and playing in white shirts, or collar-attached cotton or woollen shirts, and well-creased slacks, look both well and appropriately dressed.

Women on the Course. While sympathy is felt for those early golfers in their restrictive clothing, their discomforts seem trivial in comparison with those endured by their womenfolk.

Trespassing in a man's world, these pioneer women entered the golfing arena in the nineteenth century in high stiff collars with their full heavy skirts sweeping the lawns. Sailor hats balanced precariously on their piled-up hair and their club ribbons fluttered from these hats to give the added zest of complete loss of vision when making a swing in windy conditions. Their sleeves were so voluminous that they had to wear an elastic band on the left arm in order to get a glimpse of the ball on the tee. Their stance was severely limited by an American band which they slipped round the knees when addressing a ball. This band was called 'Miss Higgins' after its resourceful American inventor who no doubt devised it as the only means of seeing the ball.

In winter women's skirts were bound with leather so

Lady Margaret Scott in the restricting women's golfing dress of the nineteenth century.
Lady Margaret won the first Ladies' Championship in 1893 at the age of eighteen.

Captain of the 1965 Walker Cup team Irishman Joe Carr plays vivid and brilliant golf in his white cap with its green pom-pom.

that the mud could be sponged off and, as petticoats of the same length were worn, bad weather must have made golf very heavy going indeed.

Women showed unsuspected physical strength in overcoming, to some extent at least, these obstacles. Fortunately fashion relented and by the beginning of the First World War skirts were ankle-length instead of brushing the ground and women knew the bliss of a soft collar instead of the stiff throttling horror of the nineties. As the years passed, women's dress on the course became ever more comfortable and practical. Skirts became shorter and slimmer, and even divided.

The Female Revolution. Then came the most sensational development in the history of golfing wear. In 1933, Miss Gloria Minoprio shook the Ladies' Golf Union to its foundations by appearing in trousers to play in the English Ladies' Championship at Westward Ho. This was the first time a woman had ever been seen in trousers on a golf course, let alone in a Championship; but there has never been a more elegant outfit. Miss Minoprio was tall and slim and as she came striding over

the sand dunes for her first appearance—she never used the clubhouse—she made quite a sight. Clad in black from head to foot, she wore a tight-fitting sweater, slim trews anchored under her instep, and a little black cap. She used only one club, a cleek, with which she won a couple of matches. Had she allowed herself a few more clubs she might have gone far, for she struck the ball beautifully.

The courage of Miss Minoprio won acceptance for the trousered woman golfer. Now this comfortable and sensible garb is practically regulation wear, especially in cold and wet conditions. Ladies even wear shirts and shorts with knee-length stockings, which can look elegant on lithe young females. But, whilst admitting the convenience of trousers, I must confess that I much prefer to see women golf in skirts. Perhaps this is an old-fashioned preference, but slacks are so unbecoming to some women!

Diana Fishwick always chose white and always wore white gloves. A comfortable and fresh-looking ensemble.

The accepted summer golfing outfit for feminine Tournament players in the United States, its elegance depends largely on the wearer. Here it is shown to full advantage as Mrs. Marlene Hagge, a successful young professional, swings for my camera at Boca Raton, Florida, in 1956.

The incomparable caddie

In no other game has the attendant achieved such a status and importance as has the caddie in the game of golf. The relationship of caddie to player is paralleled only by that of squire to knight in the lists during the romantic days when wars were fought with pageantry and discretion.

Recognised by the rules of golf as a member of the 'side', the caddie is the only person from whom the player or players may ask advice on the club to use or the shot to play. He is regarded as an active participant to such an extent that his sins of omission or commission, such as accidentally interfering with an opponent's ball, incur the same penalties as if they had been committed by the player himself.

The word caddie had once a slightly derogatory flavour. It is a Scottish interpretation of the French 'cadet', the name given to the younger sons of French nobles who came to Edinburgh as pages to Mary Queen of Scots. From this the loafers who lined the Edinburgh streets, waiting to run errands or do any odd jobs not requiring much diligence, were referred to disparagingly by the Scots as 'caddies'.

Eventually the name became restricted to the carriers of golf clubs and the professional caddie soon denuded it of any unfortunate subservial meaning, imbuing it with respect. The new caddie's conception of his position is evident in the story of the caddie whose employer asked him to fetch a jacket inadvertently left at the clubhouse. 'Go back for it yersel'!' the caddie replied indignantly. 'I'm paid to carry, no' to fetch and carry!'

In connection with the title of caddie, it is interesting to note that the purists of golfing terminology scorn the use of the verb 'to caddie'. At St. Andrews your hench-man undertakes to carry for you; never to caddie.

Soon the caddie became a character and no annals of the game are complete without anecdotes about him, titbits of eccentricities and idiosyncrasies, like the tale of a well-known Edinburgh caddie who lectured the gallery at the beginning of an important match on the necessity of 'keepin' weel back off the greens, and giein' the players elby room'. As the game progressed and gained in excitement with each hole the crowd pressed forward, drawing in closer and closer round the pin. At the ninth hole the player succeeded in holing a tricky four-yard putt. So deep was his concentration and so near were the spectators that their resounding cheer, ringing almost in his face, gave him quite a start. The caddie was tried beyond his endurance. He swung round and gripped the ear of the nearest offender who was, in fact, a magistrate of his own town. Forcing the struggling victim's head close to the hole he bellowed angrily 'D'ye see it now? There's nae doot the ba's in the hole. But if ye're still jubious, stick yer inqueesitive nose farrer in, an' ye'll feel it.' A much subdued magistrate rejoined the crowd and the game proceeded before a very well-behaved gallery.

The earliest record of fees paid to a caddie is contained in the still-preserved household accounts of the Marquess of Montrose, which in the year 1628 noted a payment of fourpence 'to the boy who carried my clubs'. During the next hundred years fees were not raised much, sixpence a round being the usual payment. A maximum limit of this amount was fixed by the Royal and Ancient in 1771, who imposed a penalty on any player breaking this rule that he had to buy two pint bottles of claret at the next club meeting. So somebody enjoyed the penalties of extravagance.

The first caddie: Mary Queen of Scots enjoyed a game of golf, while her cadet, son of a French nobleman, carried her clubs.

A golfing scene of the 1880s. There were no golf bags then and the caddie, third from left, carried the clubs under his arm. I suppose the gentleman in the high hat was a guest, though he looks more like an undertaker.

36

This is the standard type of folding caddie cart which has replaced the caddie, for a caddie is an expensive luxury nowadays.

Who would want to wheel round his own clubs when he could enjoy his round in the company of Denise, this chic French girl caddie at the fine winter golf course of Mougins, behind Cannes on the French Riviera. The girl caddies at this famous club are renowned for their beauty and ability and several generations of the same family work at the club.

From Caddie to Professional. Some who started their golfing careers as caddies when they were boys later became makers of golfing equipment. Andrew Dickson, the first caddie whose name is recorded, caddied for the Duke of York on the Leith links in 1681 before becoming a skilled clubmaker. It is probable that this same Dickson assisted in the famous first International foursome when the Duke and his shoemaker partner, John Patersone, defeated the two English noblemen.

David Robertson, a member of the famous family of featherie ballmakers, started as a caddie and eventually became so skilled as a player and a teacher that his services were much in demand. It is very likely that his valuable coaching did much to embark his son Allan, the first great professional, on his wonderful career.

As time went on the caddie was learning to play and make money on the side, on his way to becoming the real forerunner of the modern professional, uniting the duties of club-bearer and coach. This transition from the status of senior caddie to professional came with the Robertsons: David Robertson was the last of the senior caddies, his son Allan became the first of the 'great professionals'. The caddie had become guide, philosopher and friend to the nineteenth-century golfer, ready with encouraging advice or with anxious admonition, at hand to arbitrate with the opposition caddie in all disputed strokes. His enthusiasm seemed at times to exceed that of his master. Every defeat was his personal grief and shame. And each victory . . . well, as a famous caddie once said, 'D'ye ken who really won that match? Me!'

Caddie and Captain. As he followed his master hole by hole and game by game, noting all his foibles, his strength and his weakness, and mentally mapping every trap and pitfall of the course, the caddie began naturally to regard the side as a two-man team, with himself as captain directing the player in the execution of the strokes. Typical of this attitude was the incident at the eleventh hole at St. Andrews when the caddie, having handed the cleek to the player for the tee-shot, interrupted him frantically at the top of his swing. 'Stoap! stoap!' The caddie was almost incoherent with anxiety. 'I have decided to play the shoat with my iron.'

Another favourite story shows the independence the caddie retained and which no fee could buy. A Scottish law lord, disgruntled at his caddie's failure to turn up for his regular weekly game, complained 'You know that Wednesday is my day and I expect you to keep it for me.' 'Well, my lord,' the man replied, 'I never heard of but ae lord that has a day of his ain, and I dinna keep that. I'm damned if I'm going to keep yours!'

It has often been said that caddies know everything about the game and nothing about caddying. But throughout the years, and still today, there are caddies whose expertise has saved several shots in a round. In a relationship with the player which is like a partnership, the caddie becomes so responsive to his master's game

Anthony Nelson-Keyes, the film director, rides a three-wheel motorised caddie car. An American invention, this little machine is great fun. It runs on petrol and goes like a bomb!

My electric golf buggy eliminates all the foot-slogging. I am wearing plus twos, the chic narrow version of the older plus fours.

that he can hand him the right club without a word being spoken.

A Caddie's Reward. This devotion and dedication is often recompensed. Walter Hagen gave his Open Championship prize money to his caddie, as did Gene Sarazen in 1932, and I was happy to give my man £100 when I won the title for the first time at Royal St. George's in 1934.

Arnold Palmer rewarded his caddie with one thousand dollars when he won his second Open title. Palmer did not compete in the 1964 Championship at St. Andrews and Tony Lema, making his first visit to the famous club, used Palmer's caddie and paid a gracious tribute to this famous caddie when he won the title. But when asked by an inquisitive reporter how much he had given the man he quietly replied that it was a personal matter between himself and his friend, 'but you can be sure he will be satisfied'. Which, I think, dealt very neatly with the situation.

The American Professional Tournament Bureau recommends that players should not give caddies more than 5 per cent of the prize money to eliminate any advantage being held by richer or more generous players. Also with the object of preventing rich players from buying the services of the best caddies, a draw is made to allocate caddies to players before the U.S. Open Championship. This may be an over-evaluation, but certainly a caddie who understands a player and knows the game is rare and precious.

Many great players started their golfing as caddies; learning by watching, cleaning clubs and borrowing their masters' clubs for practice. One of these was Andrew Kirkaldy, the great professional of the Royal and Ancient, who was caddie-cum-professional at the age of fifteen and beat many illustrious opponents in his day.

Good caddies still travel the country and are in demand at championships and big meetings. Leonard Crawley, who has played for England fourteen times, put his faith in Mullins, a caddie whose magpie shoes and well-cut jackets led to him being identified by spectators as one of the players. Mullins, who loves cigars, had an unerring eye for borrows on the greens and anyone who faithfully followed his instructions could be fairly sure of either holing the putt or laying it dead.

The ranks of caddies are thinned now; fees are heavy and, except on big occasions, the trolley has taken over from the caddie. But can anything substitute for the service which Rex Hartley received from his caddie in one big match. Towards the end Hartley asked for his spoon, thinking he could get nicely home with a fancy shot. But his caddie thought otherwise. He disapproved of anything that might spoil the score. 'Ye'll tak' yer iron,' he commanded, to the amusement of all, 'and hit it straight! What dae ye think ye're playing in? A pantomime?' Hartley meekly accepted the proferred iron and returned a winning score.

The Amateurs
and their game

For more than a century Blackheath was the only golf club in England. The second club was formed in 1818 on Kersal Moor by the Manchester Golfers. Even then the first three courses were laid out by Scottish exiles, Westward Ho being the first English golf club to be formed by its locals.

In these days club professionals were only a step above a caddie, many in fact performed caddie duties. The Amateurs were called 'gentlemen golfers' and were, then as now, the financial backbone of organised golf.

One thing that did more than anything to promote golf as a popular English sport was the inauguration of the annual match between Oxford and Cambridge, which became as famous as the Boat Race. This is the oldest first-class amateur golfing event in the world.

The University Match. The introduction of golf to Cambridge is credited to W. T. Linskill, a student who founded the Cambridge University Golf Club in 1873 and was eventually responsible for the inauguration of the annual University Match. Linskill appears to have been quite a vivid personality, though more enterprising in sport than in study. He had been some years at the university with no evidence of scholastic success when his parents, lonely in the long separation from their son, decided to move to Cambridge. When they died there, many years later, their son was still a popular, if unproductive, student.

The Oxford University Club was formed in 1875 and the two universities met in 1878 to play the first match in a series which is still keenly contested and which has produced many great players over the years.

In the first match Oxford scored a decisive victory, beating Cambridge by a combined total of twenty four holes in four singles matches over one round of eighteen holes. The Oxford side included Horace Hutchinson and Alexander Stuart, the best amateurs of their time.

With two such players on their team, Oxford were confident of repeating their initial victory on the Wimbledon course the following year. Cambridge arrived first at the course. They were in excellent fettle and looked gay in their red coats, the colour still worn on Wimbledon Common. The train carrying the Oxford team had broken down on the way, a common enough occurrence in those days, and they arrived hungry and dispirited. This may account for the resounding defeat they suffered at the hands of Cambridge, even the great Horace Hutchinson falling victim to an unknown player called Pattison by five holes.

The University Match was played at Wimbledon for its first fifteen years. The venue then moved to Royal St. George's, Sandwich, for ten years, until, in 1904, the universities adopted the system of playing over a different course each year, the right of choice alternating between the captains of the two sides.

The obvious defects in the method of scoring by holes were clearly shown in the result of the 1907 match.

England beat Scotland by 3 and 5 in this International Match at Westward Ho.
The English team were: Back row (left to right): S. Robinson, E. P. Storey, T. F. Ellison, The Hon. M. Scott, S/Ldr. C. A. Hayward. Sitting: R. A. Wethered, Sir E. Holderness, Cyril Tolley, H. D. Gillies.
The Scottish team were: Back row (left to right): J. Guild, E. P. Kyle, T. H. Osgood, A. F. Graham, A. Menzies, T. A. Torrance. Sitting: E. Blackwell, Robert Harris, W. L. Hope, W. H. Murray.

With only one game to go Oxford had a lead of twelve holes, but their last player was ill and finished thirteen holes down, so Cambridge were declared winners by a single hole. This marked the end of this system and the following year saw the introduction of matchplay as we now know it, with one point for each match. Heralded by the University Match, this change set the fashion for team competitions all over the globe.

Concurrent with the alteration in the method of scoring was a change in the record of results. The tendency had been for the victories to go in runs, so that in 1907 the records were level with fourteen matches each and one match halved. For the next twenty years victory passed yearly from one team to the other. Then Cambridge began to take the lead, until Oxford had a leeway of nine victories to make up in 1960. This Cambridge achievement is the more commendable because the preponderance of golfing talent was always on the Oxford side.

Amateur Champions. The double distinction of having instituted both the British Amateur Championship and the Amateur International lies with the Royal Liverpool Golf Club.

The first Amateur Championship was played in 1885. Nearly all the best amateurs took part in it, though it was not recognised as being a Championship event at that time. Its status was established in 1922, when St. Andrews accorded it recognition as the first Amateur Championship and the winner, Allan Fullarton Macfie, was retrospectively saluted as the first amateur champion of Great Britain.

At the end of the nineteenth and during the first decade of the twentieth century the dominant figure in the Amateur Championship was John Ball of Hoylake.

A January scene on one of our best seaside links. Leonard Crawley, former English champion, is putting in the annual competition played at Rye in Sussex for the Oxford and Cambridge President's putter. On this historic prize the winner hangs his golf ball by a silver chain.

Ball was eight times champion, an achievement which no player has ever equalled, nor is ever likely to equal. A very popular and unassuming player, Ball's career was interrupted by the First World War, never to be resumed as he was, regrettably, killed in action.

The resumption of the Championship after the First World War brought some great players to the fore, among them Cyril Tolley and Roger Wethered.

Cyril Tolley won the first post-war Championship at Muirfield in 1920. Dubbed 'majestic Tolley' by the Press, he could drive the ball great distances, indeed his feat at Troon in 1923 has never been equalled. At the first hole, which measures three hundred and fifty yards, Tolley drove to the heart of the green and sank the putt for a two. He also drove onto the 18th green, which measures three hundred and seventy yards, at St. Andrews, both feats being accomplished with hickory-shafted clubs.

Tolley represented Great Britain for the Walker Cup seven times, once more than Roger Wethered, brother of the equally gifted Joyce, who won the Amateur title in 1923.

Cyril Tolley on the first tee at St. Andrews.
This picture clearly shows his double-handed grip on his steel shaft, though I think he was at his best with hickory-shafted clubs. As a boy of twelve, Bobby Locke saw Tolley play in South Africa and was so impressed with his swing that he modelled his rhythm on that of the great Cyril Tolley.

In 1921 Willie Hunter from Kent, whose father was a professional, entered the Championship as an unknown to win a very decisive victory by beating A. J. Graham of Hoylake by twelve holes with eleven to play. After such a success it was not surprising that he should turn professional and go to the States, where he has since lived.

The following three years were dominated by Ernest, later Sir Ernest, Holderness, and by Roger Wethered who sandwiched his only Amateur Championship victory between Holderness' two successes. Wethered's victory was at Deal, when he defeated the favourite contender, American Francis Ouimet, in the semi-final, going on for a comfortable win over Scotland's Robert Harris in the final. Harris had his compensation by winning the following year at Westward Ho, home of the great J. H. Taylor.

Every year the American challenge was becoming more formidable until, in 1926, both the Open and the Amateur cups went across the Atlantic: the Open being won by the great American amateur, Bobby Jones, and the Amateur Cup going to Jesse Sweetser.

Relaxed grip and hands high in a Bobby Jones finish in 1927, this shows the great champion in a well-balanced position. Notice the short spiked golf shoes worn in those days.

The result of this Amateur Championship at Muirfield was a complete surprise. Bobby Jones, who was confidently expected to win the event, only lasted to the last eight, while Sweetser, who had to go to the 21st in his semi-final against the Hon. W. G. Brownlow, went on to win the title for the first and only time by comfortably beating Scotland's Fred Simpson in the final.

The cup was won back for Britain the following year by Dr. William Tweddell of Stourbridge. It was retained by T. P. Perkins and Cyril Tolley, only returning to America in 1930 in the hands of the all-conquering Bobby Jones.

This year of 1930 was Bobby Jones' year, the year that placed him among the immortals of golf with his four National successes: the American Amateur and Open Championships and the British Amateur and Open Championships.

This was indeed a grand slam: an achievement never equalled in golf. At the end of it all Jones retired completely, stepping from the top of his pinnacle with no second thoughts. With no more worlds to conquer, perhaps the rest would have been anti-climax.

The Old Course at St. Andrews was the scene of Jones' only British Amateur victory, a course which he had at first hated, but which he later came to love. He beat Roger Wethered in the final, having previously defeated several fellow-Americans who were in Britain that year for the Walker Cup Match.

The Amateur Cup returned to Britain for the next three years, via Eric Martin-Smith, John de Forest and the Hon. Michael Scott, whose win in 1933 made him the oldest Amateur Champion in British history.

The Americans returned to the scene in 1934, when Lawson Little won and held the cup for two successive years. Little has two claims to distinction: he was the first American to win the Championship on a first attempt and he won with the biggest margin ever when he beat James Wallace by fourteen holes and thirteen to play. It was a fine win for Little, but an unexciting finish for the crowds who invaded Prestwick that afternoon. In his second win the following year Little had a harder fight when he was taken to the 36th hole by Dr. Tweddell.

A long-awaited win for Scotland came in 1935 when Hector Thomson put out Jim Ferrier, the first Australian

A fine Amateur, Dr. William Tweddle was a real weekend golfer who decided to play in the Amateur Championship during his annual holiday. He made golf history, becoming Amateur Champion in 1927 and finishing as runner-up in 1935. He used a hollow-headed wooden putter, seen here, with deadly effect, often from miles short of the green.

Golf among the houses: the first hole at St. Andrews with powerful Irish Amateur Cecil Ewing playing a pitch to the green. Ewing played championship class golf for over thirty years.

to reach the final. Thomson needed a half to win on the 36th green at St. Andrews and he pitched over the Valley of Sin so close to the hole that he was not asked to putt.

The Championship was won by a Californian-English player, twenty five year old Bob Sweeny, at Sandwich in 1937, when he beat fifty year old Irishman Lionel Munn in the final. The cup was retained for America the following year by Charles Yates, who defeated Irishman Cecil Ewing, many times a Walker Cup player in a championship in which the entire defeated U.S. Walker Cup team competed.

In the last Championship before the war Alec Kyle, a Scot who lived in Yorkshire, defeated Welsh International Anthony Duncan at Hoylake.

Champions of Recent Years. The first post-war Cham-

pionship, at Birkdale in 1946, was won by the twenty five year old long-driving Irish star, Jimmy Bruen. As a lad of nineteen Bruen had led the qualifiers of the 1939 Open Championship, and there is no doubt that he was destined for many golfing victories. It was indeed a tragedy when his left hand was crushed in an unfortunate accident, bringing a brilliant career to a premature end.

Two American years followed with the victories of Willie Turnesa and Frank Stranahan. Stranahan, known as 'Muscles' was twenty six years old when he won his first British title. He had great strength and spent hours exercising to develop and strengthen his arms and legs. He was indefatigable and would practise until darkness after every match. In his first British success Stranahan defeated Charlie Stowe, the greatest Midlands golfer of his day, and the following year at St. Andrews

P. B. Lucas, one of the best-ever lefthanded golfers. Lucas was at Cambridge University, which he later captained. After a brilliant war record in the Air Force he began to play again in 1946 and captained the Walker Cup team when it visited America in 1949.

Two champions: Frank Stranahan and George Duncan. Son of an American spark plug manufacturing millionaire, Frank was a regular visitor to Britain after the war and he won the Amateur Championship in 1948 and 1950 before turning professional in 1954. He plays little golf now, but he still manages to get in the prize list.

Ronnie White playing in 1946, when he was twenty five years. This fine golfer dominated the Amateur scene from his schooldays until his retirement from big golf, though he never won the Amateur Championship.

A champion in action. Joe Carr, triple Amateur Championship winner, drives off.

he beat his American colleague Dick Chapman. Stranahan, a very rich man, turned professional in 1954 and seldom visits England now.

In 1949, another year with a strong American entry, the volatile Irishman, Sam M'Cready kept America at bay by defeating Chapman at Portmarnock. But Chapman had his turn when he beat Charlie Coe, the thin man of American golf, at Royal Porthcawl, and it was another all-American final when Harvie Ward beat Frankie Stranahan in his last bid for the title at Prestwick in 1952.

Many times winner of the Irish Open Amateur title and the greatest of the Irish amateurs, Joe Carr stepped in at Hoylake in 1953 to take the Amateur Championship Cup from Harvie Ward and win the first of his three Amateur Championships.

A magnificent stylist now, he altered his natural short swing slashing action after winning two of his Championships. Carr bubbles over with vitality and makes friends at every hole. He has played in many Walker Cup matches and is now captain of the 1965 Team—after leading the 1964 Great Britain and Eire Eisenhower Trophy Team to victory in Rome. Winner of the Amateur at St. Andrews again in 1958 and again in 1960 at Royal Portrush, he won his Irish title for the fourth time in 1964.

The first Commonwealth Tournament was held at St. Andrews in 1954 to celebrate the bicentenary of the Royal and Ancient. It was fitting that this should be Australia's year with a win at St. Andrews and a victory for their leader, Douglas Bachli, in the Amateur Championship at Muirfield.

From the States in 1955 came Joseph Conrad, to win at Royal Lytham. The following year a British youngster named John Beharrell created golfing news by becoming the youngest ever Amateur Champion and the first English player to win since 1933. Eighteen years old, Beharrell played with all the sagacity and courage of a veteran. An added strain on the young golfer was the increase that year to thirty six holes for the last three matches, but he came through with flying colours. Beharrell beat Reid Jack, a Scot who had accounted for Conrad in the quarter-final, and he met and defeated another Scot, Leslie Taylor, in the final.

Reid Jack, who represented Scotland in the Internationals eight times, won the Championship the following year, beating American H. B. Ridgley at Formby.

The final of the Championship in 1959 was an all-American one – always depressing for Britain – with D. R. Beman beating W. Hyndman at Sandwich.

After the joyous interlude of Joe Carr's victory in 1960 came the great victory of Michael Bonallack. Bonallack had a fairly easy passage on the Ailsa course at Turnberry, never playing more than sixteen holes. When he faced Ayrshire's James Walker in the final he set about him with four under fours for the first twelve holes. There was only one answer to that.

46

At eighteen, John Beharrell became the youngest-ever Amateur Champion in 1956.

Reid Jack, Amateur Champion in 1957, using an iron for his second shot.

American Deane Beman won the Amateur Championship in 1959.

47

The Cup went to America in 1962 via R. D. Davies, but the following year Michael Lunt, brilliant son of a famous English Champion, won at St. Andrews. He had been knocking insistently at the Championship door and his win was a very popular one.

The Unexpected Champion. The winner of the 1964 Championship surprised everyone, even himself. Thirty one year old Gordon Clark from Whitley had entered mainly because the venue was at Ganton in his own county. In common with many others he did not rate his chances highly. On his way Clark defeated American Walker Cup player, Dale Morey, who had disposed of Michael Bonallack. Clark then proceeded calmly to the final in which he deposed the holder, Michael Lunt. So the man who expected to be an 'also ran' became instead a giant killer.

Michael Bonallack, one of today's top amateurs, winner of the 1961 Championship.

Concentration paid off for Michael Lunt when he became Amateur Champion in 1963.

In the 1964 Championship.

The
Walker Cup

In the era of dawning internationalism between the two world wars three great international contests were instituted between Great Britain and the United States in a most successful bid to stimulate golf interest on both sides of the Atlantic.

The idea for the Amateur International Championship was initiated by George Herbert Walker of the National Golf Links of America, who offered to donate an International Challenge Trophy. Announcing this, the newspapers called it the 'Walker Cup' and this name has stuck. It was originally decided that the contest would be an annual affair but this placed a very heavy financial strain on amateur golf resources, so it was finally agreed that the event should be held biennially.

The Royal and Ancient sent a team to compete in the first Walker Cup match at Long Island in 1922. Though they were defeated, the British team secured four points out of the twelve, one of their best efforts. It is sad, but a fact, that since the beginning of the competition the British Isles have only succeeded in winning once; the only other occasion when success seemed within grasp was at St. Andrews in 1926 when the United States succeeded by the narrow margin of one match.

The British win came at St. Andrews in 1938, when they ended the American string of nine successive victories. It was a memorable occasion, witnessed by people ten-deep behind the white posts on the historic golfing stage of the Royal and Ancient.

Hero of the match was eighteen year old Irish discovery, Jimmy Bruen. The youngest player ever to be chosen for the Walker Cup team, Bruen was also chosen to lead the team on both days, an unusual honour but also a terrifying ordeal.

In the crucial match of the foursomes Bruen and Harry Bentley were three down to Charles Kocsis and Johnny Fischer after eighteen holes. Fischer, forgetting he was playing in a foursomes and having missed a short putt, unthinkingly knocked the ball into the hole. The American referee asked the Britishers if they would claim the hole but they refused and the half left them still three down.

They were still two down with three to play. The crowd watched in silent excitement, tensely counting each loss and gain. A pin-splitting second from America produced an even better one from Bentley, and Bruen holed the winning putt on the 16th. Bruen got on the narrow green at the 17th, but Koscis was in the long grass fringing the dreaded road. The crowd were right behind Bentley, in spirit, as he made the next shot, hoping he would lay the 25 yard putt dead. He did better: he holed it for all square, and that halved match gave the foursomes to Britain.

Inspired by this success and by the old tradition, not always proved by events, that the team winning the foursomes wins the match, Britain set out confidently on the eight singles of the second day. They won five of them to

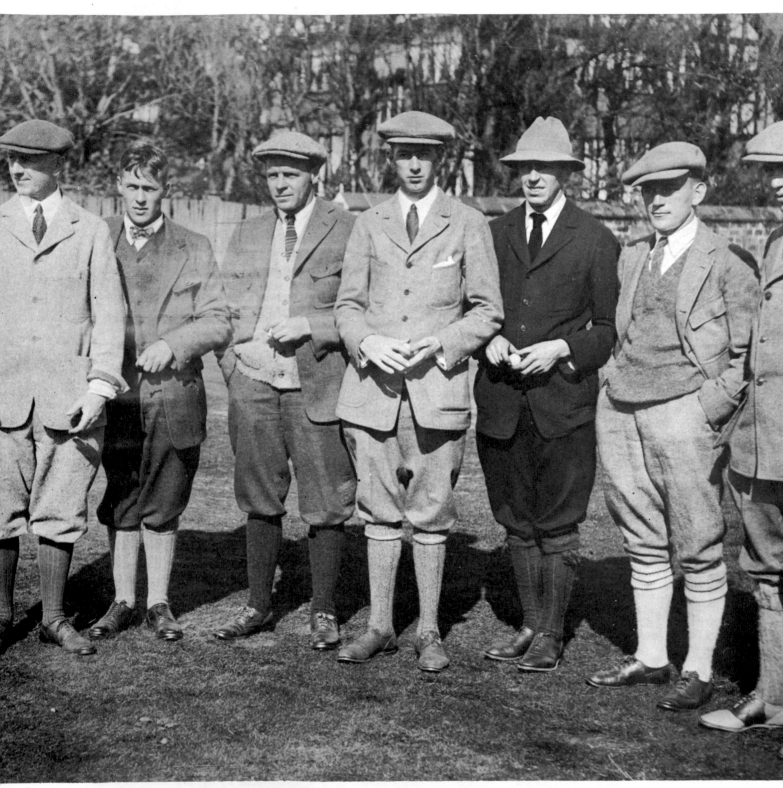

*An American team which came to Hoylake to play a British team in 1921,
the year before the Walker Cup match was instituted. The players are (left to right): Jesse Guildford, Bobby Jones,
Fred Wright, Wood Platt, F. Ouimet, Paul Hunter and W. C. Fownes.*

The successful British Walker Cup team 1938. Front (*left to right*): Harry Bentley, Cecil Ewing, John Beck (*captain*), Charles Stowe, Jimmy Bruen. Back (*left to right*): Gordon Peters, Hector Thomson, Leonard Crawley, Alex Kyle, Frank Pennink.

The unsuccessful American Walker Cup team of 1938. (*Left to right*): Marvin Ward, Fred Haas, Charles Yates, Johnny Goodman, Johnny Fischer, Ray Billows, Charles Kocsis, Reynolds Smith.

John Beck and Francis Ouimet, captains of the British and American Walker Cup teams of 1938.

make the victory seven matches to four, with one halved. Bruen led the team against Charles Yates but, not surprisingly, this experienced player was too much for him. He fought bravely from three down at the half-way stage to lose by only two and one; had he not missed a couple of short putts he might well have squared.

But the British tail wagged magnificently to win the last three matches. Two Scots, Hector Thomson and Gordon Peters scored personal successes. Both perfected the art of shooting inside the American ball on the greens; it is a pity they could not have handed on this skill to the men who have followed them.

A. T. Kyle, winner of the Amateur Championship the following year, made victory assured when he beat tall Fred Haas by five and four. In their thousands the crowd rushed off to see the last match of the day; not a decisive one, now, for Britain was now holder of the Walker Cup for the first, and only, time. But this was still an exciting game, with Irishman Cecil Ewing fighting Ray Billows every inch of the way and giving the ecstatic spectators full measure by winning on the 36th green.

The British captain, John Beck, had succeeded in imbuing a miscellany of individuals with a unity of spirit which proved individual. Beck's happiness was complete when the news was received of Mrs. Baba Beck's simultaneous win in the Irish Championships at Portmarnock.

With the intervention of the war it took a decade for the United States to regain the Cup, but they succeeded at St. Andrews in 1947 by eight to four. The match has continued each second year with no further success for the British Amateurs.

Dubliner Joe Carr, Walker Cup player and triple winner of the Amateur Championship. A powerful golfer who lives for the sport, Joe trains assiduously in a manner which would shame most professionals and amateurs. Originally a long driver, Joe altered his grip completely some ten years ago and improved still further his play by this drastic change.

The beginning
of the Open

The contest for the Challenge Belt, inaugurated in 1860 by the Prestwick Golf Club in Ayr, was the first organised annual Open competition for professional golfers. The first meeting was open to professionals only, but this restriction was removed the following year to allow amateurs to compete. The original charter of the championship in 1861 declared the competition 'open to all the world' and, in principle, this still applies.

The Championship was played at Prestwick for the first eleven years, and as the course was then only twelve holes the Championship was decided over thirty six holes, three times round the course. The champion Belt was an elaborate affair of red morocco, richly ornamented with massive silver plates and costing the then handsome sum of thirty guineas. It could be retained by any player winning the competition in three consecutive years.

Little enthusiasm was evoked by the contest, which had only eight entrants in 1860 and did not increase notably during the next few years. It seemed destined to peter out, as the earlier Amateur Championship had done, when on to the scene came Willie Park of Musselburgh and 'Old Tom' Morris of St. Andrews. The rivalry between these two men excited fresh interest in the event, and this enthusiasm has gained impetus ever since. Of the first eight Championships Morris won four and Park three, their monopoly of the event being interrupted only by Andrew Strath's victory in 1865, the sixth year of the competition.

'Young' Tom Morris. In golfing skill, however, 'Old Tom' was outshone by his own son 'Young Tom', the finest golfer in Scotland at that time and indeed one of the greatest golfers of all time. Born at St. Andrews in 1851, 'Young Tom' was only nine years old when the first Championship was played. He entered the arena at the age of sixteen and finished fourth, but in the following year he achieved the first of his four successive victories by which he won the Belt outright and established a golfing record that has never been equalled before or since. His total of 149, achieved in his 1870 victory, knocked twenty five strokes off the score of Park ten years earlier and for the three years which won him the Belt he was on average nine strokes better than the runner-up. It has also been calculated that on the par of the course 'Young Tom' was two strokes more than perfect play for his thirty six holes. He played shots to the greens with backspin and accuracy that would be admired today. Had he lived there is no doubt that he would have gained very many further honours on the course; but he died at the age of twenty four on Christmas Day, 1875.

'Young Tom' was buried in the Cathedral churchyard at St. Andrews, and a bas-relief figure representing the young man, almost life-size and instinct with golfing dash and power, depicts him addressing the ball in an iron shot. His grave is a yearly mecca for golfing visitors in their thousands and the American Ryder Cup teams

'Old' Tom Morris, one of the first golfing heroes in the gutta ball days. He won the Championship Belt, which was the first award for the Open Championship, in 1861, 1862, 1864 and 1867, when there were only eight to ten entries for the event.

A better player than his father, 'Young' Tom Morris wears the coveted Belt, which he won four times in succession, in 1868, 1869, 1870 and 1871, when it became his property. Sixteen opponents were the most he had to encounter in any of these matches, though this is no way detracts from his remarkable skill at the game. After the Belt had been won outright a Cup was substituted and Young Tom was the first winner in 1872. This is the same elegant trophy which is played for today, though it now has two plinths on which are inscribed the names of the winners. Young Tom died at the age of twenty four, never having recovered from the loss of his young wife, who died in childbirth the same year.

Golfers from all over the world pay tribute to Young Tom Morris at this memorial in the cemetery of St. Andrews Cathedral. It is considered an essential part of the visit to St. Andrews, which is the aspiration of every golfer. A smaller memorial stone was added to the grave when Old Tom Morris died, many years after his son.

never fail to make the pilgrimage. He died tragically young, but his fame lives on.

The New Trophy. After the outright winning of the Belt, a new Championship trophy in the form of a Silver Cup was presented for play and this became the permanent trophy of the event. The first contest for the Cup, at Prestwick in 1872, gave 'Young Tom' his fourth successive victory.

It was now decided to rotate the event over the courses of Prestwick, St. Andrews and Musselburgh and this had the immediate effect of attracting a larger entry. The first contest at St. Andrews had the unprecedented field of twenty six.

The champions for the next eleven years were all Scottish professionals, but in 1890 John Ball, a famous amateur of Royal Liverpool, beat all the leading professionals of the day to become the first amateur to win the Open Championship.

One of the greatest amateur players, Ball, is still spoken of with reverence in his native Hoylake where his father owned the Royal Hotel across the road behind the 17th green. This hotel, now demolished, was the first headquarters of the Royal Liverpool Golf Club, which began as nine holes over the Hoylake rabbit warrens in 1859, and which is today one of the great Championship courses of the world, on which all the great golfers have played.

Besides Ball, Hoylake produced another great player in Harold Hilton. A few years older than Ball, he soon became his rival and went on to win the Open Championship at Muirfield in 1902, over a Championship course which had been extended to seventy two holes since 1892. Hilton was again winner on his beloved Hoylake in 1907, and in 1911 he became winner of the American Amateur title to complete his golfing success.

The victories of the Royal Liverpool amateurs, John Ball and Harold Hilton, presaged the end of this early period of Scottish monopoly in professional golf. In 1894 J. H. Taylor became the first English professional to win the Championship played on an English links for the first time and this opened a new vista in the development of the game.

The Great Triumvirate. 'The great Triumvirate' they were called: Harry Vardon, James Braid and J. H. Taylor. Professionals all, they won the Championship sixteen times between them and dominated the scene, with hardly an interruption, until the First World War.

Harry Vardon's record of six Open Championships has never been equalled, whilst the great James Braid and J. H. Taylor each won the Championship five times. James Braid was born in Elie, Fife, and played as an amateur until 1896. Taylor and Vardon had already won the Open Championship when Braid turned professional, but he was the first to win five times. His rise to fame was meteoric, from his first win in 1901 he completed his quintuplet in ten years, besides winning

the Matchplay Tournament four times and countless other honours.

He refused repeated invitations to visit the United States and compete in the American Open, which he would undoubtedly have won. After eight years as professional at Romford, Essex, he went to Walton Heath and remained there as professional for forty five years. During his last twenty five years there, he was accorded honorary membership. Two months before his death, he was made a life member of the Royal and Ancient Club, as were J. H. Taylor and W. Auchterlonie, professional at St. Andrews. A man of few words, big gentle James Braid was never at a loss when a decision was required. One of the founders of the Professional Golfers' Association he was a dominant figure at all the big meetings at Walton Heath. Once during the *News of the World* Matchplay Championship, Braid was controlling the huge crowd when a ball caught the full skirt of a woman on the edge of the 18th fairway with such force that it wrapped the skirt tightly round her legs. She stood petrified until Braid, striding majestically up, took her by the shoulders and twirled her round until the ball fell on the grass. This earned him the gratitude of both the woman and the thankful player who, saved from all penalty, hit a magnificent shot to the green.

John Ball poses in his last years with the steel shaft, to revive the memories of those who knew him in his great days.

55

Harold Hilton, winner of both the Amateur and Open Championships, was an artist with the golf clubs. Though very far removed from the power golfer of today, with his sensitive fingers and loose grip he could really make the ball obey him. His golfing costume is typical of the early part of the twentieth century, with shallow starched collar, plus fours and jacket in jersey material.

Watched by Harry Fernie, by tee box, the great Harry Vardon drives off. With waistcoat and medal showing is J. H. Turner, Frilford Heath, one of the great golfing characters of his day and a popular club professional.

'The Great Triumvirate' in their heyday: Vardon, Taylor and Braid, now alas all dead. They are playing with spliced-headed wooden clubs and wearing the conventional jackets of the day. Vardon always wore knickers, but Braid and Taylor never favoured them. This is a composite picture, the background crowd having been pieced in for atmosphere at a later date.

Prior to 1893 the Open champion received £5 in prize money. This was increased in 1892, so that in the days of the Triumvirate a cash prize of £30 was awarded to the winner, as well as a gold medal. In order to make a living the Triumvirate used to travel the country playing exhibition matches for varying sums. Sometimes the sum was quite considerable. One famous match fetched £400 in fees. In this game Braid played with Sandy Herd against Vardon and Taylor. Herd had the enviable distinction of achieving nineteen holes-in-one during his golfing career. But a new era in Championship golf was now approaching with the advent of the American conquerors.

The great J. H. Taylor in his ninetieth year.

The Open
between
the wars

The birth of organised golf in the United States took place in 1888. Golf had been played before then but, as in the early days of the game in Britain, there were no clubs and no competitions. The first club to be formed was named St. Andrews, in honour of the Scottish club which is the world's golfing embassy and the spiritual home of all golfers.

By 1900 there were over one thousand golf courses scattered throughout the United States, every state having at least one course. But although golf was firmly rooted, it was still in its infancy and for many years was dominated by players from Scotland and England. It was not until 1911 that the U.S. Open Championship, started in 1895, was won by a 'home-bred' professional, J. J. McDermott, and on at least one occasion both of the fighting finalists were British.

In the second decade of the twentieth century America's new stars were just beginning to shine and their meteoric progress was not halted much by the outbreak of war, their major tournaments only being cancelled during the 1917 and 1918 seasons. In Britain all serious golf was suspended from the end of the 1914 season until 1920. But though the impact was severely felt, the first season after the war found British golfers still sitting on top of the world, with Britain's Ted Ray winning the U.S. Open title and another Britisher, thirty six year old George Duncan winning the 1920 British Open Championship. Abe Mitchell, who had turned professional only the previous year, looked set fair for the title, with nine strokes in hand at the half-way stage, but the mercurial Duncan, famed for his high-speed play, pranced round Deal in dazzling figures on that last day and defeated Mitchell. In the succeeding years the names of Duncan and Mitchell were coupled as they became what the pre-war Triumvirate had been to Britain: travelling around together, entering contests as a pair and playing exhibition matches.

Nineteen-twenty-one was the year when Roger Wethered robbed himself of the Open at St. Andrews. He was leading in the final round when, at the 14th green, he walked backwards while studying the line of his shot and trod on his own ball. The penalty shot cost him the Championship, for instead of winning outright he tied with Jock Hutchinson, a Scot resident in the U.S., and lost the replay.

Enter the American Conquerors. Now came the time when the pupils turned masters, a period which was ushered in, most fittingly, by the great American show-man, Walter Hagen. Though the precious Cup has been claimed by the United States many times since this 1922 Championship, Hagen holds the record of being the only American to win four times: in 1922, 1924, 1928 and 1929. Never at a loss, Hagen was an amazing player and a diabolical putter. Possessing no sense of time he would cause everybody else palpitations by dashing on to the tee at the last moment, with no time even for a practice

Golfing in the 1920s seems to have been inducive of comradeship and good cheer, if one can judge from this photograph of Sandy Herd, 1902 champion; J. H. Taylor, five times champion; James Batley, golf professional and Harry Vardon, six times champion. Notice the narrow starched collars, standard golfing fashion for professionals of that day. I have tried playing in such a collar and found that it allows for very free movement of the head within its cool frame, not being inclined to cling and stick. The natty tiepins and clips of these old-timers adds up to a picture which provides a sharp contrast with the often slovenly dress of many players today.

Five great golfing personalities pause for a chat on the 1st tee at Roehampton Golf Course in London, shortly after the end of the First World War. Fred Robson talks to pipe-smoking Ted Ray, while a trio is formed by Tom Williamson, George Gadd and Arthur Havers. A very popular golfer with a real sense of humour, Robson was a real golf stylist. He and Ray travelled hundreds of miles playing a great number of matches together. George Gadd and Arthur Havers also made several golf tours together and were a popular pair wherever they played.

swing; but he could retrieve a rank bad shot by holing a putt right across the green.

In a seventy two holes exhibition match at Moor Park before the 1928 Championship Hagen was defeated by Archie Compston, our leading player at that time, by the unbelievable margin of eighteen up and seventeen to play. He had only just arrived in England when he played this match, but he managed to acclimatise himself in time to win the Championship. In those days it meant a very long week on a rolling ship to come to Britain from the United States.

A ten-year run of American victories began with Hagen's second win in 1924. Robert Tyre Jones, the greatest American amateur of all time and in the opinion of many the best player ever born, won three times, the only amateur to win the Open since Harold Hilton in 1897. Bobby was a glorious free swinger of the hickory-shafted club and was never the same player when he turned to steel shafts.

The Tide Turned. Arthur Havers in 1923 registered the last British victory in the Open until I had the honour of turning the tide in 1934. The winners during these

Ted Ray, a Channel Islander from Jersey, was one of the great golfing characters of his day. He hit the ball vast distances with an ungainly style, but he had a velvet putting touch with an aluminium-headed putter.

Tom Webster, the great sporting cartoonist, always depicted Ray as a figure buried in deep rough with smoke issuing from his pipe to betray his whereabouts. This used to annoy Ted, or so he said. 'I'm a straight driver really, mate' he used to say.

George Duncan had a curious putting grip. He was never a reliable putter but loved to experiment and would try any form of grip and all types of club. After one quick look at the line he would give the ball a sharp tap. One of his favourite clubs was called a 'meat axe' by his colleagues, because it had a very deep square blade with some loft on it. The ball 'took off' on a long putt.

Percy Alliss, father of Peter and Alec, was a great golfer in the period between the wars, and won many big events. He was a stylist but never a great putter; had he putted like Palmer or Locke he would never have been beaten, for there have been few strikers like him. He is seen here at the finish of a drive with the hickory shafted club he used so well.

George Duncan drives off in a game played in the immediate post-war years. A great stylist, George was renowned as the fastest professional golfer, barely taking time to get his stance before beginning his back swing. He was an 'inspirational' player: given a good start he would continue brilliantly, but a bad start would often make him sulk. Notice the dress of the mainly male gallery and the old-style elevated tee box, with sand for teeing up the ball.

Golfers of the twenties: left to right, George Gadd, Dr. William Tweddell, Michael Bingham and Arthur Havers, in the days of the hickory shafts. The golfing dress of this period did not include open-necked sports shirts; these came later. George Gadd was an International player. Dr. William Tweddell, a phenomenal putter, was Amateur champion of 1927. Michael Bingham was a long driver but never a good tournament player, he had a poor competitive temperament. Arthur Havers, Open Champion of 1923, was a powerful golfer with a fine tournament record.

Macdonald Smith, born in Carnoustie and settled in America, and Tom Fernie from Scotland, playing in the Open Championship at Prestwick in 1925. The caddie follows with six wooden clubs in his bag, while the players carry their hickory-shafted irons. 'Mac' Smith, a wonderful stylist and successful tournament player, was another 'great' who never succeeded in winning an Open title.

Arthur Havers won the Open in 1923 and determined to show the American visitors that we had at least one Britisher who could play golf; but somehow he was never quite able to reproduce the form of his great year, when he was just twenty three years old.

American years were Walter Hagen, Jim Barnes, Bobby Jones, Tommy Armour, and Gene Sarazen, while in 1933 the British doldrums were intensified by an all-American play off at St. Andrews, when Densmore Shute beat Craig Wood in the replay after a tie.

I am very happy to say that my Championship win at Sandwich was far more than a personal victory; it provided the impetus from which British golf took a grand new lease of life, which lasted right up to the Second World War.

This was my eighth attempt at the Championship, but I had set it as my target for even longer than this.

My prescription for good golf was then, and has always been, work and harder work. While I was playing, the game became all-important to me so that I was oblivious of my surroundings: 'Concentration Henry' Walter Hagen dubbed me.

So it meant quite a lot to me when I opened my bid with a first round of 67, which tied with Hagen's first round when he won his fourth Open Championship in 1929. Excitement went sky high when I followed this with a 65. On the third day the Championship was nearly washed out. The 7th green was under water but the green staff managed to sweep it away as the storm sub-

This is the bunker on left of the dog-legged 17th hole at Royal Lytham and St. Anne's Golf Club, into which Bobby Jones, 1926 Open Champion, put his drive in the final round with Watrous. Jones carried the intervening rough and low hills to the green and finished nearer the hole. Watrous three putted, lost the hole and the championship.

Bobby Jones in his best playing years, 1921 to 1930. Immaculately yet soberly dressed, this popular young amateur from Georgia, U.S.A., set a great example, on the courses of the world.

Friends and rivals, Walter Hagen and Gene Sarazen. These two great American golfers enjoyed playing up the story that they hated each other, rather like the Hope and Crosby team. Regular visitors to Britain, their names are inscribed in the history books of the game on both sides of the Atlantic and golf owes them a great debt. Both elegant dressers, they set the pattern in money-making for the stars of today.

A plaque marks the bunker made famous by Bobby Jones in the 1926 Championship.

Gene Sarazen, Open Champion 1932, driving at Trent Park, London, in 1937.

One of the great players who never won the Open,
Archie Compston is seen here playing a pitch shot.

The Open Championship at St. Andrews in 1933:
the great 'Haig', Walter Hagen, strides out, carrying his
curved shafted hickory putter, and accompanied by
Amateur Rex Hartley. The styles favoured by this great
champion had a great influence on the dress of the day.
Hagen's elegance makes today's golfers look very sloppy.

Walter Hagen fishes in a lake at Gleneagles Hotel, watched by the course ranger in deer-stalker hat. Now
around seventy years, Hagen still loves this peaceful pastime.

sided and I finished in 72 to keep still far ahead of the field with a lead of eleven shots.

The last round was the most uncomfortable of my career. I suffered an acute attack of stomach cramp, caused, no doubt, by tension and nerves. Added to this I developed a hook which I couldn't correct until I turned for home. But as the pain eased and a good putt went down on the 13th green I recovered form to finish in 79 for an aggregate of 283. This gave me a win by five strokes from S. F. Brews of South Africa. My second round of 65 – never before achieved in the Championship – gave the name of Dunlop 65 to the golf ball which I used at that time and which is now famous the world over, still carrying the number.

Victory remained with Britain for the next five years. In 1935 Alfred Perry won at Muirfield by four strokes, though the bookmakers had offered him at sixty to one! He was a slashing player who took all sorts of risks, even using a spoon from a bunker, and his confidence on the greens contributed to his win.

A tempestuous and very closely fought Championship in 1936 saw Alfred Padgham emerge victor, to make it a golden year in which he won almost all the big events. A thunderstorm caused play to be abandoned in the afternoon of the first qualifying day and there was little improvement in the weather the following day. On the final day Padgham arrived on the course with time for a few practice swings only to find the professional's shop locked with his clubs inside. After unsuccessful attempts to find somebody with a key, Padgham eventually had the window smashed and a small caddie climbed in to rescue his clubs. He just managed to reach the first tee in time to avoid being disqualified for unpunctuality. Apparently quite unflustered, Padgham began play with his characteristic lazy, graceful swing, and finished winner by one stroke. The runner-up was Jimmy Adams, who was dubbed the champion runner-up for the number of times he came within an ace of winning big events. This Championship marked the debut as an amateur of the Great South African Bobby Locke, though it wasn't until 1949, when he had been a professional for years, that he won the title.

Championship Weather. I had my second Championship win on the giant course of Carnoustie in 1937, when

Open Champions both: Denny Shute (right) in 1933 and Sam Snead in 1946. There is a very rare early photo of Sam, one of the world's greatest golfers, before he became bald at a very early age. 'Slamming' Sam has made a fortune from golf with his powerful and rhythmic swing.

Taken in 1933, this photograph shows my characteristic drive: with braced left side and firm grip on the follow through. In 1934 I was privileged to be the first home player to win the Open since Arthur Havers in 1923. My win broke the American hold on our title.

Alfred Perry, an unorthodox golfer, who won the Open Championship in 1935. Perry's great golf on the difficult Muirfield course produced a surprise win. Here he is recovering successfully from a deep sand bunker. With the club held in the palm of his right hand, Perry just addressed the ball with an unusual casualness and then 'belted it' with all his strength, the club shaft sliding about in his right hand.

A drive from Alfred Padgham, winner of the 1936 Open Championship at Hoylake. Fifty nine year old Padgham has now retired from the game through ill-health. A great putter and a remarkable judge of distance, he always allowed his head to follow the clubhead much more than many top players, as can be seen here. Padgham had a favourite steel-bladed putter with a yellow sheathed steel shaft which he seemed to swing as if he were driving, holding his arms away from his body, even for the short putts.

R. A. Whitcombe, who was the only member of the famous golfing family to win the Open. The youngest brother of the Whitcombe trio, Reginald was a fine attacking golfer who used the interlocking grip, popularised again recently by American Champion Jack Nicklaus.

Trying to see the bright side, the exhibitors at the 1938 Open Championship pose in front of the wrecked Exhibition tent. The tent and all its contents were destroyed during the night's gale which preceded the final day's play. The gale continued through the final games, making scores rocket.

Two of golf's great ones pause on the 18th green at St. Andrews after a practice round before the Open Championship of 1936. Sandy Herd, Open Champion 1902 and Jack White, Open Champion 1904, were both still fine players even in their old age.
Sandy Herd was professional at Moor Park for many years and Jack White reigned at Sunningdale.
Sandy repeatedly 'beat his age', even in tournament play. He was the only player I have ever seen using the double handed palm grip. He was famous too for the large number of waggles, often eighteen, he made before deciding to begin his back swing.
Jack White was the first golfer to break 70 in the Open Championship.

the opposition included the whole might of the U.S. Ryder Cup team. As I had never seen this great public links, I paid a brief pre-match visit to acquaint myself with the famous Barrie Burn which winds about the course.

With one round to go I was three strokes behind the leader, Britisher Reggie Whitcombe. It was probably the wettest day in the history of the Championship. The wind blew and the rain swept across the course from the sea, putting holes under water so that fresh ones had to be cut on higher surfaces. It seemed sometimes as though play would have to be abandoned, but still we played on. At the last hole, where most of the field played short of the Burn which crosses the fairway just before the green, I hit the ball as hard as I could and as far as possible from the out-of-bounds on the left. My shot carried the Burn and finished hole-high in a bunker on the right, I got out of the hard wet sand safely short of the hole because there was an out-of-bounds beyond the pin, and got down in two putts on that sodden water-logged green. I finished the round in 71 to win by two strokes.

Reg Whitcombe had his revenge the following year at Sandwich in a Championship on which the sun shone until the final day, when gales tore the Exhibition tent to fluttering ribbons, when golf balls were frequently blown backwards and it was actually possible to lean on the wind. There was no better score in the third round than Whitcombe's 75 and he finished early with a final round of 78. In my final round I was out in 36 in this howling tornado and I started home 4, 3, 3. A 71 would have resulted in a tie but I could only manage a 74, which was, incidentally, the best score of that day. I finished third, with Jimmy Adams retaining his role of champion runner-up. Reg Whitcombe was the youngest of the three brothers who made such a mark in British golf and the only one of them to win the Open.

The Unlucky Champion. Richard Burton has always been considered the unluckiest of Open champions, for his success came in 1939 and the outbreak of war prevented him from reaping the benefit of his win. Burton had a tremendous tussle and it was anyone's Championship until his last round of 71 beat American Johnny Bulla by two strokes, though Bulla had the second best last round with 73. Burton finished like a champion. He hit a drive of nearly three hundred and fifty yards at the last hole, played a delightful niblick shot on to the green and holed the putt for a three.

The setting was St. Andrews and the finish tense and dramatic: the perfect stage and the fitting curtain to twenty years of golf between the wars.

Richard Burton, Open Champion 1939, in action at the Lotus Professional Golf Tournament at Stoke Poges. Burton was a fine free swinger of the club.

The Open
after the Second
World War

Once more the din of battle faded and the drone of planes overhead was replaced by the swish of a golf ball travelling through the air as the round of Championships and Tournaments began again.

At first it did not seem as though golf in Britain had suffered through the long years when clubs gathered dust in cupboards and men's minds were fully occupied with a grim game in which they could not afford to be losers. In the immediate post-war years the amateurs who had been prominent before the war still looked good and professionals acquitted themselves well in tournaments. But it soon became obvious that in neither the amateur nor the professional ranks were there any young players of talent who could replace eventually the pre-war leaders. After seven golfless years there were two hundred and twenty five entries at St. Andrews in 1946 when the Open was resumed. 'Slamming' Sam Snead had a hard fight for victory to take the Cup back to America, having won by four strokes with a score of 290. The Championship was still wide open with one round to go. Snead, American Johnny Bulla and Britain's Dai Rees were level and I was one stroke behind. I was still suffering from the ill-health which had caused my discharge from the R.A.F., and as I grew increasingly tired towards the end my chances faded. Bulla found the road at the 17th and Rees had a tragic 80. South African Bobby Locke, who was just coming into the picture again, tied for second place with Bulla.

First Irish Champion. Fred Daly of Balmoral, Belfast, became the first Irishman ever to win the Open when he confounded the critics at Hoylake in 1947. This Championship ended on a dramatic note. Daly had finished his last round with a ten-yard putt for a three and American Frank Stranahan, then an amateur, sent a tremendous second shot to the final green which rolled to a few inches of the hole. Had it dropped in he would have tied with Daly.

A Triple Champion. Muirfield in 1948 was the scene of my third Championship win when, with a total of 284, I beat the previous champion, Fred Daly, by five strokes. The long carries and narrow fairways of this course suited me to perfection. After hard training I was in the peak of form and a second round of 66 set me on the way to victory.

This was the first Open Championship ever to be watched by a British monarch and when King George VI walked with me for a number of holes, this second round became known as 'the Royal round'. I decided to retire from Championship golf there and then; I felt I had been fortunate to win, and wanted to end my playing days on a high note.

Bobby Locke Returns. Having come close to winning the Open in 1939 and 1946, Bobby Locke's win at Sandwich in 1949 was a popular one, though sympathy was felt for the Irish runner-up Harry Bradshaw who experienced the most amazing of all Championship mishaps.

Bradshaw's first round of 69 led the field and he was doing well in the second until he drove his ball into the rough at the 5th and found it lodged in the bottom of a broken beer bottle. The bottle was lying on its side and the ball must have crept into it with its last roll. Bradshaw did not know what to do. Someone reminded him of the rule which stated that 'the ball is unplayable if the player considers that he cannot make a stroke at it and dislodge it into a playable position'. But Bradshaw was still uncertain as to what he should do, and finally the spectre of possible disqualification made him decide to play the ball where it lay.

Closing his eyes because of the danger of flying glass he sent the ball about thirty yards with his blaster. The hole cost him a six and unsettled him. Ill-luck followed him the next six holes and he finished the round in 77.

But with the famed Irish resilience Bradshaw regained confidence to do his next two rounds in 68 and 70. With a total of 283 he tied with Locke but in the play-off Locke went round in 67 and 68 and Bradshaw, overstrained, was beaten by twelve strokes.

Two years after this incident a new clause was added to the rules which permits the player, if he considers his ball unplayable in accordance with the definition, to drop a ball under penalty of one stroke in both match and stroke play. A ball is considered 'unplayable' if the player considers he cannot make a stroke at it and dislodge it into a playable position. Now a free lift is allowed from such 'outside the game' objects.

Bobby Locke retained his title the following year at Troon, always a difficult thing to do, and his total of 279 was four strokes better than the previous record held jointly by Sarazen, Locke, Bradshaw and myself. He gained a slight advantage by the fact that this course was only six thousand five hundred and eighty three yards then, by modern standards a little short for a Championship course. It has now been lengthened to over seven thousand yards. Locke emerged a worthy champion after a period of disaster, which started at the 5th and culminated at the 8th hole. This hole is the famous 'Postage Stamp' which is surrounded by deep sand bunkers. Locke hooked his tee shot to the left of the green; he exploded out into another deep bunker with his second shot. At the risk of repeating the performance he played his third shot for the flag. The gallery, no less than the player, were tense with anxiety as the ball landed safely on the green, sat there and allowed Locke to hole it for a four.

Fred Daly, winner of the 1947 Open at Hoylake, was the first Irishman to win this coveted title. Fred hit the ball vast distances from the tee with a long heavy driver, but it was his short game and particularly his holing out skill which brought him his successes.

I hold the historic trophy for the third time, having won the 1948 Open at Muirfield with a total of 284, including a record round of 66. The medal, seen here in its box, I had converted into a brooch for my wife; my previous two medals had been made into a bracelet for her. I think it is better to use them thus than to store them.

King George VI followed my 66 round when I won the Open at Muirfield in 1948. This was the only occasion on which a reigning British monarch has followed a Championship. His Majesty was accompanied by a crowd of officials, with Dai Rees, extreme left, and Norman Von Nida, on his right, as guards.

Dai Rees of Wales watched by Flory Van Donck of Belgium during play in the 1948 Open Championship at Muirfield. Rees, now a senior professional, still gives the young players plenty of tough competition.

Norman Sutton watches Flory Van Donck of Belgium hole a putt on the 13th green at Muirfield in the 1948 Open Championship. Sutton later won the world's senior professional title. Van Donck has been a consistent money winner for years. Even now, when well over fifty years, he continues to beat the youngsters all over Europe.

Locke resumed the round with admirable calm and finished without further mistakes.

Max Faulkner, our most colourfully garbed player, won at Portrush the following year and his has been the last British victory to date.

The Cup Travels. Bobby Locke's win in 1952 was the beginning of a period when the effect of the long golfless years hit British Championships.

The 1953 Championship went to America with the great little Ben Hogan who won with consummate ease at his first attempt on the massive course of Carnoustie, reducing his score with every round and totalling 282.

Australian Peter Thomson, who was runner-up to Locke in 1952, achieved his first of three successive wins in 1954, the first player to achieve the trio since Bob Ferguson of Musselburgh did it in 1880, 1881 and 1882. Thomson's victories were on Royal Birkdale, St. Andrews, and Hoylake.

Bobby Locke won his fourth Open at St. Andrews in 1957 with a total of 279. His last round of 70 could not be beaten and he won from Peter Thomson by three strokes.

The Australian golfing wizard Thomson returned the following year to gain his fourth Open title at Lytham and St. Anne's after a tie with powerful David Thomas. They played together on the last day and Thomas was in the lead with two holes to play when he played a crooked second at the 17th which brought the scores

Ben Hogan, with his wife, Valerie. Four times winner of the U.S. Open and 1953 winner of the British Open, Hogan is a golfing perfectionist and one of the most accurate strikers of the ball of all time. He received very bad injuries in a car crash in 1948 when, seeing that a head-on collision with a bus was inevitable, he dived across his wife to save her. He made a marvellous recovery and can still show young players how the game should be played.

Max Faulkner, last home winner of the British Open Championship in 1951. Faulkner never made the game look easy; he always thought it could not be right to play easily. Here he marks his ball before a huge crowd at the Sunningdale Golf Club, watched by a successful Scottish golfer John Panton. Faulkner has now accepted an appointment to manage a 'stable' of young players, financed by a London business man with the object of winning major golf championships.

A giant of a man still in his early twenties,
David Thomas became famous after his clash
with Peter Thomson in the 1958 Open Championship,
when he lost on the play off. He is a fine tee shot
player, has a great temperament and has already great
experience. He putts well, his only weakness being the
short pitch. I like the elbows forced together here
prior to impact.

Gary Player, another young amateur from South Africa
who has become one of the game's top professionals,
being top money winner in the U.S.A. in 1961, and winning
the British Open Championship in 1959 at the age of
twenty four. Only five feet seven in height, Player
has built himself into a golfing giant by continual
physical training. Not a stylist but a fine strong
player with great determination, he has already made
a fortune from golf and hopes to retire before he is
thirty five years of age and bring up his four children.

equal. Thomson ran away with the thirty eight holes replay by four strokes.

South African Gary Player won at Muirfield in 1959 and this was a win gained by sheer determination. He was eight strokes behind the leader at the half-way stage. He made up four of them with one round to play and with a final round of 68 he won by two strokes. Flory Van Donck might have caught him right up to the end for, six under fours on the last tee, Player drove into the massive bunker on the left and wound up with a six. Van Donck needed a three to tie but his second was short of the green and he took five.

Australian Kel Nagle was champion in 1960 in the Centenary Open at St. Andrews, and America's Golfing Great, Arnold Palmer, in 1961 and 1962.

Gales and floods accompanied the 1961 Championship at Royal Birkdale when Palmer won with 284 with gallant Ryder Cup captain, Dai Rees, who is surely the greatest home player who has never won this title, only a stroke behind him.

Australian Kel Nagle, winner of the 1960 Open Championship at St. Andrews, hits an iron shot to the 16th green.

Arnold Palmer forcing the ball from semi-rough during the 1961 Open at Royal Birkdale.

79

An exciting player to watch, Arnold Palmer plays a wonder shot to the holeside during the 1961 Open. He went on to win by two shots. The faces of the crowd register anxiety; they were shocked when his third shot went flying across the green into the rough. He made an unusual five at this hole, putting this shot near the hole.

A scene at Royal Birkdale during the 1961 Open Championship: one of the few occasions in the past forty years when play in a big event was called off. This was the night the tents blew down on the area behind the clubhouse. Sheltering behind his umbrella, Ralph Moffitt had started exceptionally well, but the heavy rain had flooded the greens and once any hole is under water golf is impossible. My umbrella had blown inside out. I had a towel tied in my umbrella and another in my belt to try to keep my hands and grips dry. But the wind drove the rain everywhere so that even our waterproof clothing was no protection.

Arnold Palmer played one especially wonderful round in the 1961 Open at Royal Birkdale, playing in a gale which overnight had demolished the tent town behind the clubhouse. This is the scene on the plot behind the club the next morning as workmen set about tidying up the site.

Palmer created a new Open Championship record at Troon in 1962 with his total of 276. Throughout the week he seemed to put almost every shot from about forty yards dead and, with his wonderful putting, outstripped everyone. Kel Nagle was six strokes behind and the leading home player, Brian Huggett, was thirteen strokes in the rear.

Australian Bob Charles made headlines in 1963 when he became the first left-handed player to win the Open. For this achievement they dubbed him 'Charles the First'. A dedicated player who spends every possible moment in practice, Charles had played in the United States during the five months preceding this Championship and he also became the first left-handed player to win a big event there.

On his first visit to England and in very rough conditions Tony Lema, one of America's top money-spinners, won the 1964 Open at St. Andrews with a great score of 279, including one round of 73. We used to cherish the illusion that high winds would baffle the Americans. The gales that blew across the Old Course at St. Andrews in 1964 swept with them all these false hopes, as they

A television tower near the 6th green at Troon during the 1962 Open. Australian Peter Thomson watches his
ball roll towards the hole while Harold Henning of South Africa squats, waiting his turn to putt.
Until recently there has been little coverage of golf on television as the authorities considered it
lacked viewing appeal. As the game increases in popularity this view is gradually changing. The camera can get
some fine shots from these elevated stands.

A crowd rushing for vantage points near the green at the 16th hole at Troon, when following Palmer and Nagle in the last round of the 1962 Open Championship. First to the green get the best view.

Peter Thomson pushing through firmly from the semi-rough at Troon in 1962.

Arnold Palmer putts, with his much copied knock-kneed stance, at the 1962 Open Championship at Troon.

American Phil Rodgers holes a putt which led to the tie with Bob Charles for the 1963 Open at Royal Lytham and St. Annes. Rodgers likes to clown; he dropped his cap over the hole and his putter on the ground when the ball dropped in.

Spectators with periscopes gain viewing advantage at the replay between Charles and Rodgers in the 1963 Open at Royal Lytham and St. Annes.

Lefthanded New Zealander Bob Charles shakes hands with Phil Rodgers whom he defeated in the play-off for the Open title at Royal Lytham and St. Annes in 1963. Charles made history by becoming the first 'south paw' to win one of golf's great titles. He is a very fine player who made his name as an amateur when working as a bank clerk in New Zealand. He has continued to shine and he is the world's first 'leftie' champion.

After the presentation: Bob Charles and his pretty wife clasp the famous old trophy. A proud day for them both!

eliminated the British chief hopes with Neil Coles and stalwart Peter Alliss failing to qualify. Bernard Hunt, of similar physique to Alliss, fought the tempest and finished in fourth place.

The gales affected Lema, as indeed they did every player on the course, but they did not prevent him from qualifying. He had come a long way to make acquaintance with St. Andrews, he said, and he wanted to see plenty of it. He also liked the small ball, which tamed the wind for him, and he continued to use it when the easier conditions allowed him to take the lead with a second round of 68. He retained his lead firmly to finish with a final round of 70.

Lema celebrated his win, as he always does, by inviting everyone within earshot to join him in a victory drink of champagne. His celebration bills would be enormous were it not for the fact that they are subsidised by a champagne firm; naturally Tony holds the bottle with label to the fore when being photographed pouring out the 'bubbly'.

So the Cup continues to go overseas. But I think there is hope that in the years ahead some of the young players will take up the challenge and reassert Britain's supremacy on the links, but to achieve this we must play with the larger ball.

The Rewards of Victory. The eight professionals who, in 1860, took part in the first contest for the Open Championship were competing purely for the honour and glory of wearing the Championship Belt; there was no other prize then. In the fourth year of the event small prizes were awarded for the runners-up but it was not until 1864 that a prize of £6 was provided for the winner in addition to the Belt. In 1893 an entrance fee of ten shillings was instituted and the half dozen clubs that constituted the Championship rota contributed to make the prize money up to £100. Out of this the winner received £30 and a gold medal.

Seventeen years later the total sum was increased by £25 and the winner's prize was raised to £50. Through the years it was occasionally increased, but even in 1931

One of the most successful money winners over the past ten years, tall Bernard Hunt was fourth in the 1964 Open, but he has yet to win the famous title. He has a great temperament and his short, rather flat, swing is under perfect control all the time.

Tony Lema hugs the famous trophy as he is presented with it for his great golf in the 1964 Open at St. Andrews. Lema went on to win the TV World Championship from Ken Venturi, Bobby Nicholls and Arnold Palmer. He pocketed 17,800 dollars for his 36 holes of golf. What money there is in the game today!

the whole amount was only £500 and that was divided into twenty-three prizes. The prize money stayed at £100 up to the intermission caused by the Second World War, though the number of contestants continued to increase, attracted less by the monetary reward than by the honour and glory of winning this great event.

When the competition was resumed in 1946 the prize list was raised to £1,000, quite a considerable amount in those days. Because of the increased burden of costs borne by players another £500 was added to this figure in 1949.

The prize list swelled to £2,500 in 1953, the winner getting £500, and in 1955 the Australian Peter Thomson became the first Open champion to receive £1,000. The previous year Thomson had received £750 for his win.

Thomson netted a very nice sum from his four wins at this peak period.

For the Centenary Championship in 1960 the prize list soared to £7,000 and another Australian, Kel Nagle, benefited to the extent of £1,250.

A still more impressive prize list of £8,500, with £1,500 for the winner, was presented for the 1964 Open Championship at St. Andrews, while in 1965 it is £10,000 with £1,750 to the winner.

This enormous increase in prize money has been made possible by the growing popularity of golf as a spectacle sport. There is little doubt that this trend will continue for there is much enjoyment to be gained by spectators as they follow their favourite champions on a fine day round the rolling courses of Britain.

Will Jack Nicklaus, the American golfing prodigy, win our Open? He has been third and second in his two tries. He wants to win this title badly and says he will keep coming over until he succeeds.

The
Ryder Cup

The professional matches for the Ryder Cup were preceded in 1926 by an earlier contest of a semi-official nature between representatives of the American and British Professional Golfers' Associations, which was won by the British on their native shores. Following this highly successful exhibition, Samuel Ryder of St. Albans, a keen supporter of British professional golf, donated a solid gold trophy bearing his name to be competed for in a series of matches between professionals of these two nations, to consist of one day of foursomes and a second day of singles matches; a third day of four-ball matches is now included.

As in the Walker and Curtis Cup matches the event is played alternately in each country. This arrangement is very fair as the character of the courses and the weather conditions give a definite advantage to the home players. While the British players wilt in the sweltering heat of an American summer, the United States players feel even less enthusiasm for the damp and often cold splendour of an English spring or autumn. After 1965 the match will take place just prior to the Open Championship in each country. The first Ryder Cup match was played in the United States in 1927 when America won by nine matches to two. The great George Duncan, Open champion of 1920, was the only singles winner for Britain.

During the ten years from 1924 to 1933 American golfers held a monopoly of the British Open Championship, but British professionals remained undefeated in the international matches on their own side of the Atlantic, though they never succeeded in winning the match in the United States.

Then in 1937 the U.S. professionals scored their first Ryder Cup win in England, and Britain did not succeed in getting the Cup back again until 1957. Since then America has been on top again so that now another British victory is long overdue.

There have been occasions when Great Britain has nearly won. We nearly claimed victory at Wentworth in 1953 when I was non-playing captain, having played in the team on three occasions. I had the team fighting fit, having trained them hard and organised their meals with plenty of prime steaks which was not easy to do as, although the war had ended eight years earlier, meat was still rationed.

Two young players who have since become famous, Peter Alliss and Bernard Hunt, were appearing in their first Ryder Cup match that year and I put them strategically in the tail. The side had already won four of the eight singles and both these stalwart youngsters appeared to have victory within their grasp. Peter Alliss put up a magnificent fight against Jim Turnesa and lost by a bare hole when, through strain, he fluffed a chip to the last green. Bernard Hunt would have won his match against Dave Douglas had he holed a tiny putt on that last green. He knew he had to win to halve the match with

Some early Ryder Cup players. Sitting are Ted Ray, J. H. Taylor and George Duncan. On the left, standing, is Abe Mitchell and next to him Harry Vardon, while the tall figure second from right is Alex Herd.

The British Ryder Cup team which was defeated at Wentworth in 1953. Back row (left to right): John Panton, Jimmy Adams, Bernard Hunt, Eric Brown, Harry Weetman, Peter Alliss and Harry Bradshaw. Sitting (left to right): Fred Daly, myself, Max Faulkner and Dai Rees.

Fred Daly holes a vital putt on the 18th green at Wentworth to give the British Isles its only foursomes point in the Ryder Cup match of 1953. Daly was partnered by Harry Bradshaw and both players won their singles matches the following day.

Ryder Cup 1953: Dave Douglas walks across the green to shake hands with Bernard Hunt who has just missed the six foot putt which resulted in Hunt halving this important singles match with Douglas.

America, as Allis had known that if he could pitch dead and win that last hole it would mean victory for the British Isles. It was just too great a strain and responsibility on such young shoulders. The United States had won the foursomes by three matches to one, but they only won the Cup that year by six matches to five with one halved.

A British Victory. In 1957 Dai Rees captained the British team at Lindrick, Yorkshire. Things looked hopeless at the end of the first day when America had won the foursomes by three matches to one. After the debacle Dai Rees said a few words of encouragement to his team. This action was suggested to him, he said

afterwards, when he remembered how impressed he had been by the pep talk which I had given to the team at Wentworth.

The following day the Americans learned that the old adage that 'the side that wins the foursomes wins the match' was not always true.

Never was there such a change of fortune. By mid-morning British hopes were soaring and, as the glad news spread, thousands poured on to the course which soon rang with British cheers. Our players were tuned to concert pitch and at the half-way stage they were leading in five of the eight matches. Scottish Eric Brown, who led the side, beat Tommy Bolt 4 and 3; Peter Mills,

Wentworth, October 1953: Lloyd Mangrum of the successful American team makes a humorous speech after receiving the trophy.

The Yorkshire scoreboard showing Britain leading at the start of the second day's play. There were many hours to go before we finally emerged victorious and at this time the excited crowd were out watching the play, hence the deserted scoreboard.

The winning British Ryder Cup team of 1957.

Arnold Palmer at the finish of an iron shot during the 1961 Ryder Cup match at Royal Lytham. Palmer is not a classical swinger, he hits the ball hard and 'to hell with how it looks'. The fairways are fenced in to keep the crowds back.

playing for the first time, beat the American captain Jack Burke 5 and 3, while Dai Rees trounced Ed Furgol 7 and 6.

Britain won the singles by six matches to one with one halved, giving them a seven to four match victory in the Ryder Cup.

Since then the old sorry story has resumed. There have been changes, eighteen holes matches instead of thirty-six, entailing changes of opposition; but the Ryder Cup has remained in the United States since the Americans recaptured it in 1959.

There is a change in the system of selection of the British team for 1965, when the match will be played at Royal Birkdale, and as the bigger American ball has been used in most events during 1964 it may be that Britain will start on more level terms. This large ball demands more accuracy than the smaller British ball and must be struck with perfection; this, I am sure, is one of the reasons why American top players are such confident and reliable golfers.

The American Ryder Cup team at Royal Lytham and St. Annes in 1961.
Standing (left to right): Bill Collins, Doug Ford, Don Finsterwald, Art Wall, E. Casper, Gene Littler.
Sitting (left to right): Jay Barber, Jay Hebert, Arnold Palmer and Mike Souchak.

The Tournament scene

The oldest of all the professional tournaments is the *News of the World* Matchplay Championship and the cut and thrust of matchplay makes this one of the most interesting professional tournaments of the year.

The competition originated in 1903 with a prize fund of £200, which was handsome in those days. The promoters increased the prize money to £400 in 1911 and to £590 in 1919. Players were encouraged with continual increases until, in 1925, this became the first event to top £1,000 in prize money, which increased later to £1,250.

Although this was the only major matchplay event of the year it was regarded only as a Tournament until in 1946 the P.G.A. gave it official recognition as the Professional Golfers' Association Matchplay Championship. The proprietors of the *News of the World* then stepped up the prize fund to £2,000 and, with constant increases, the money had increased to £3,000 by 1955, with £750 and a replica of the Cup going to the winner.

The prize fund for this competition is now £5,020 of which the winner gets £1,250.

This title is prized next to the Open Championship and the entry list is always formidable. Sectional qualifying has been replaced by thirty six holes stroke play on the two courses of Walton Heath prior to the Championship. The sixty four leaders go forward into the competition.

The winner of the opening event in 1903 was the great James Braid, who won the title four times. Of the Triumvirate, J. H. Taylor won twice and Harry Vardon once. Many great names of those early days are inscribed on the Cup: Sandy Herd, George Duncan, Abe Mitchell and the brothers Charles and Ernest Whitcombe among others.

Alfred Padgham had his first success in 1931 and he won again in 1935.

I reached the final of this competition when I was very young in 1928 and I won the title in 1932. Eight years later I won again and my third victory was on the majestic course at Hoylake in 1946.

Gallant little Dai Rees won the title for the first time in 1936 and he had his second win in 1938. When he defeated me in the final at Walton Heath in 1949, this was his third win. His fourth victory was in 1950.

The longest match of the whole Championship was recorded by Fred Daly, winning for the third time in 1952. This was in the third round at Walton Heath when he eventually defeated Alan (Tiger) Poulton at the 30th hole! This win on the twelfth extra hole still stands as the record for the British Isles.

Since then Australian Peter Thomson has taken the Cup home a couple of times, but it has mostly stayed in England.

The great Irish star Christie O'Connor won in 1957, powerful Harry Weetman the following year, and another heavyweight who believes in the value of American

Tent town at a golf tournament in Scotland. Tents provide all sorts of facilities for players and spectators and are part of the modern golfing scene all over the world. This scene shows the tasteful way the tents can be planned and on the right can be seen the end of one of the huge and very essential car parks. Only clubs with large areas of free ground near the clubhouse can house the big events of today.

£200 OPEN PROFESSIONAL GOLF TOURNAMENT

PROMOTED BY

WM. GIBSON & CO., LTD., KINGHORN,

WHO ARE PROVIDING THE WHOLE OF THE PRIZE MONEY.

WILL BE HELD OVER

The Golf Links, Kinghorn, Fife,

ON

Tuesday & Wednesday, 14th & 15th June 1921

---

36 Holes by strokes.

18 Holes to be played each day.

Partners to be drawn.

1st Prize, **£50**; 2nd, **£40**; 3rd, **£30**; 4th, **£20**; 5th to 10th, **£10** each.

[P.T.O.

At the age of twenty I made one of my early appearances on the Tournament scene, partnering Mrs. J. R. Mason, wife of the well-known Kent County cricket captain, in a foursome at the old Foxgrove Golf Club, Beckenham. The course, one of the prettiest, in the London district, was not far from Langley Park Golf Club, where I began my first full professional job. My brown and white check sweater and brown plus-fours with matching socks were high fashion then. I was even described as 'our best-dressed professional'.

A big Tournament of 1921, played over 36 holes. The prize of £200 offered then is worth at least £1,000 today, possibly more.

In 1928, at the age of twenty one, I played in the News of the World *Matchplay Championship at Stoke Poges, Bucks, and reached the final for the first time. I won the title three times, in 1932, 1939 and 1946, and played in six finals of this event. I have gripped my hickory-shafted niblick right down the shaft for this tricky stroke. Among the spectators just behind me, and also in plus-fours, is George Gibson, one of the great supporters of professional golf in Britain and animator of the successful Co-operative Association the professionals operate.*

Some of the keen and successful competitors in pre-war Tournaments. Left to right: Don Curtis, Jimmy Adams, Commander R. T. C. Roe, secretary of the P.G.A. for 25 years, Charles Whitcombe and Percy Allis.

Young A. D. (Bobby) Locke from South Africa came on the golf scene in Britain as a slim young amateur in 1936 and amazed everyone with his poise, his huge hooking flight in all shots and his magical putting. He later turned professional and came back after the war to win four Open Championships.

experience, David Thomas, won in 1963. At one time there were several tournaments sponsored by newspapers. They have dropped out over the years leaving only the *News of the World* Championship which gains in stature every year.

The Dunlop Tournament. Established in 1946, the Dunlop Masters' Tournament is eagerly contested not alone for the honour and glory its winner gains, but also for the £2,000 in first prize money.

There are only forty competitors in this exclusive field, comprising the winners of the season's important events, the Open Champions of the past ten years, Master Golfers of the same period and overseas reigning Champions, including those from America, South Africa and Australia.

The match is 72 holes strokeplay, and it has been won by Australian Norman Von Nida and by South African Bobby Locke. Irish star Christie O'Connor won in 1956 and 1959 and Bernard Hunt, top prize winner of 1963,

included the Masters' title in his great year of triumph. In 1964 the Masters' Tournament was played over three days for the first time and the venue was Royal Birkdale, again for the first time. The total prize money was over £5,000, the winner receiving £2,000. Many considered that this was too big for a first prize, making a bad distribution. Young South African Coby Lagrange hit the £2,000 jackpot.

A New Tournament. The Piccadilly World Matchplay Championship was instituted at Wentworth in 1964 with prize money totalling £16,000. The winner's share was £5,000 and every player in the tournament, each a golfing star, received some share in this prize fund, ranging from a minimum of £1,000 upwards.

This most exclusive field was limited to eight leading golfers of the world who were chosen on their achievements in world golf; I hold the course record at 64 from 1936.

The World Championship was held over the long West

South African champion Sid Brews, myself and Bobby Locke during the £500 challenge match sponsored by the News of the World *at Walton Heath in 1938. I was partnered by R. A. Whitcombe (not shown) and we won an exciting match over 72 holes by 2 and 1.*

Another scene from the News of the World *Tournament at Walton Heath, with Bobby Locke putting. Also in the picture are my regular caddie, Ernest Butler, and, on the right, James Braid who refereed the match.*

Fred Daly from Belfast, 1947 Open Champion and a fine all-round golfer with a great Tournament record. Note his very personal type of grip on the club.

Norman Von Nida, the colourful Australian who made a great impact on British golf just after the war. Though he dominated our golf for several seasons he never attained his ambition to win the Open Championship. Eventually the strain wore down his nerve and he retired from big golf in the 1950s.

Colourful Max Faulkner, Open Champion in 1951 and a wartime physical training instructor, is still a tough fit golfer in his forties. He enjoys tournament golf more nowadays since his successful operation for stomach ulcers in 1963.

One of the top playing professionals of the past decade, Peter Alliss was leader of the Order of Merit in 1964. Still in his thirties, Alliss is one of the game's big hitters. He played in the 1953 Ryder Cup side which lost at Wentworth by the barest margin.

course and as a prelude the Piccadilly £4,000 Tournament was played on the East course. Even this field was fairly exclusive, for only seventy competitors were eligible for the seventy two holes event: the sixty leaders of the Order of Merit for the season and ten players invited by the promoters.

The World Championship was won by the great Arnold Palmer who beat Neil Coles in the final by 2 and 1. Coles, a lionhearted golfer who will surely win the Open soon, had previously beaten Tony Lema, the 1964 Open champion.

These events, held in October, wound up a heavy and remunerative season for professional golfers. The British season in 1964 had a golden harvest of nearly £100,000 which in 1965 has risen to £120,000. Yet this is paltry in comparison with the American total for their all-the-year circuit which now stands at £1,000,000, meriting its title of the 'Gold Dust Circuit'.

I drive off in a practice round, watched by Tom Haliburton, then my assistant. A successful club and tournament professional and recently a Ryder Cup player, Haliburton is professional at the famous Wentworth Club in Surrey, scene of many International and Open tournaments.

A first tee scene at a small tournament in America. Note the loudspeaker on the tree, the television mast on the right back, and the coloured caddies waiting in the background.

At the Rediffusion Tournament held at the Moye Golf Club in Jersey I saw the scores of the competitors marked against par, the American procedure; really in fact against the Standard Scratch Score as we have no strict par yet. The lines of figures against the players' names showed, in different colours, how many over or under par. This makes it very easy to see who is leading at any particular moment of each round and is a form of scoring which I think will come to stay.

Ladies of
the links

From Mary Queen of Scots, charged at her trial with so much lack of decent feeling that she played golf after the death of Darnley, to the Scottish fisher lassies at Musselburgh two centuries later, women seem to have been interested in golf almost from its inception. But their active participation was frowned upon by convention and discouraged by successively cumbersome fashions of such elaborate drapery that they allowed only minimal movement.

But, formidable though they were, these obstacles were easy conquests compared to the active unwillingness of men to share their favourite sport. 'If they choose to play at times when the male golfers are feeding or resting, no one can object', said Lord Wellwood in the Badminton Library. 'But at other times—must we say it? They are in the way.'

So women must be content to stand and admire. But Lord Wellwood didn't like them as spectators either. 'If they could abstain from talking while you are playing, and if the shadow of their dresses would not flicker on the putting green while you are holing out, other objections might perhaps be waived.' No doubt he preferred to acquaint his womenfolk personally of his heroism and hardships on the links rather than have them as either opponents or critics.

Women who persisted in playing against the wishes of the lords of golf did so at the risk of being branded witches, a fate that befell Dame Margaret Ross, wife of the Earl of Stair. She was accused of beating her golfing opponents by using her evil powers to convert herself into the other player's ball which then showed a striking lack of co-operation and allowed Lady Margaret an easy win.

Nowadays we have to invent other excuses when our balls turn into enemies! But women carried on playing and making plans of their own, though it was not until the second half of the nineteenth century that the first ladies' clubs came into being. The earliest of these was the St. Andrews Ladies' Golf Club. The Royal and Ancient seems to have led the field in giving encouragement to these women pioneers and the St. Andrews Ladies' Golf Club was the first to be formed in September 1867. But even then women were relegated to links of their own, much shorter than men's courses, which were generally provided for them by some of the bigger clubs.

Independence for Women Golfers. The formation of the Ladies' Golf Union and the inauguration of the Ladies' Championship in 1893 begins the modern history of women's golf. This was the start of the formation of ladies' clubs which were entirely independent of the men's clubs, having their own clubhouse and often their own course.

The Ladies' Golf Union rules women's golf throughout the world and has done so for more than fifty years. It has gained the admiration of the golfing world by the way

A beautiful swing from Joyce Wethered in her heyday. Her woollen two-piece features the long skirt of the period. In wet conditions this could become a burden and a handicap.

Joyce Wethered plays a delicate pitch and run. A picture taken in the late twenties, when skirts had shortened and cloche hats were fashionable.

in which it has governed its ever-extending empire over the years, and considerable credit accrues to Miss Issette Pearson, who formed the union and who also contributed much effort to the running of the first Championship. The winner was eighteen year old Lady Margaret Scott, who repeated her success in the following two years.

The gradual establishment of a national system of handicapping was the biggest achievement of the Ladies' Golf Union. Though it has been modified since this was still a sound, workable system and reasonably reliable from club to club. The system of handicapping was chaotic even in men's golf at this time and these comparative newcomers to the game set an example of reform which the men had perforce to follow.

Meanwhile Irish women launched their native Championship at Carnalea. When the Ladies' Golf Union held their meeting at Portrush in 1895 some of the young Irish players watched the great Lady Margaret Scott win her last competition, for after this contest she retired unbeaten, never again to take part in any serious contest. The strength of her game inspired the Irish Hezlet sisters and Rhona Adair. May Hezlet won three times in the space of nine years, and her last success in 1907 was against her sister, Florence, whom she defeated 2 and 1 in the final at Newcastle, County Down.

Two Golfing Queens. In 1914 when the great Cecil Leitch won her first Championship she wore a less-restricting ankle-length skirt and knew the bliss of a soft collar instead of the stiff throttling horror of the nineties. A great golfer, and a tremendous personality, Miss Leitch was then seventeen and had never had a lesson in her life. She had played from childhood on a strip of turbulent course on the edge of the Solway Firth with the wind blowing from all directions: one would have to be a good golfer to fight and conquer such conditions and Miss Leitch struck the ball with a crispness and ferocity that amazed the spectators. She won the Championship three times and reigned supreme among women golfers until the entry of Joyce Wethered. The rivalry between these two champions dominated the women's golfing world in the succeeding years.

In 1921 Joyce Wethered and Cecil Leitch clashed in the final of the Championship at Turnberry and Cecil Leitch emerged winner by 4 and 3. But the following year the two met again and Joyce Wethered became champion by the overwhelming margin of 9 and 7. But Miss Leitch was not easily crushed.

They met again in the 1925 final at Sandwich in one of the greatest women's games ever fought and Cecil Leitch took Joyce Wethered to the 37th hole before acknowledging defeat. When it was over Joyce Wethered cried with regret at having to inflict defeat on so brave an adversary.

Cecil Leitch and Joyce Wethered each won the Ladies' Open Championship four times. Playing with her famous brother, Roger, Joyce Wethered won the Worplesdon

'Di' Fishwick, who was very popular with the crowds, holes a good one. Her putting action seemed all in one piece, like a wooden doll, but it was very successful.

A fine impact study of Enid Wilson, with Open Champion Alfred Padgham in the background. Enid Wilson won the Ladies' Amateur Championship three times in succession before retiring to become a professional and, later, a successful journalist.

Enid Wilson receives her third Amateur Cup at Gleneagles Hotel after having beaten Diana Plumpton in the final.

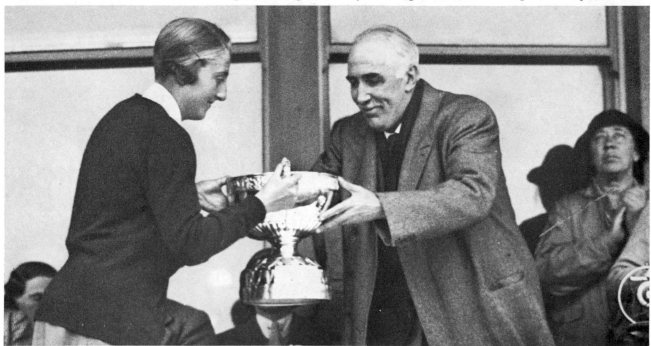

Mixed Foursomes in 1922, the first of her eight wins in this event with different partners. She also reached the final in 1938 with her husband, Sir John Heathcoat Amory.

Competition from Abroad. Golf on the Continent was thriving, and in the two years preceding Miss Wethered's last Open victory in 1929, the title went to France. Miss Wethered celebrated this last occasion at St. Andrews by defeating the first of the American invaders, Glenna Collett, who was again beaten the following year at Formby by nineteen year old Diana Fishwick who started out lightheartedly with the remark 'What a lark, I am Britain's white hope'.

Then came Enid Wilson's three victories in a row. At this period there was no one to touch her and she might have gone on winning for years but at the age of twenty-three she retired to become a professional and later a successful journalist.

The title remained in Britain for the next six years, with seventeen year old Pam Barton, one of two gifted Surrey sisters, reaching the final in 1934 and again the following year.

Her year of triumph came in 1936 when she won both the British and American titles, the first player to do this since 1909. She was again British champion in 1939. Shortly after this she became a Flight Officer in the

A large gallery watches the 1947 Ladies' Amateur final on the beautiful Scottish course at Gullane, overlooking the Firth of Forth. In this match one of Scotland's leading golfers, Miss Jean Donald, was beaten 7 and 5 by Mrs. Mildred Zaharias (America's Babe Didrickson).

W.A.A.F., and she was killed on active duty in 1943. The second post-war Championship, in 1947, went to Mrs. George Zaharias, who took the title home at her first attempt. She outdrove everyone at Troon that day. An outstanding sportswoman, she was voted Woman Athlete of the Year on five occasions and before she was seventeen years old she had established three world's athletic records in the 1932 Olympic Games, which earned her nickname 'The Babe'.

Mrs. Zaharias turned professional shortly after winning the British title and she won the World's Championship, Tam O'Shanter, in four successive years. Later she visited England with a team of women professionals and with Patty Berg she ran a golf clinic where, apart from teaching, they entertained the crowds with their amazing trick shots.

The British Ladies' Championship Cup again travelled to America in 1948 with Louise Suggs, who, like her illustrious predecessor, turned professional after her win. Frances Stephens, daughter of a professional, regained the Cup for Britain in 1949 and became our leading woman golfer for a number of years. She celebrated her marriage to Roy Smith in 1954 with another Championship win. She captained the British Curtis Cup team in America in 1962 and has a highly successful record in Curtis Cup matches.

Pam Barton, golfing prodigy of the 1930s, a freckle-faced, cheery redhead who loved, indeed lived, golf.
She made all sorts of golfing history, even beating the Americans on their home ground. She was so good that even on an off day she could hold most of her rivals and when she hit top form she could romp home to victory.

An all-round athlete who found golf an easy game, America's Babe Didrickson was better known as 'The Babe'. Babe married George Zaharias, an all-in wrestler. As an amateur she won all the top golfing honours and when she later turned professional she 'cleared up' the proettes. Tragically Babe died of cancer when quite young.

'Bunty' Stephens, now Mrs. Frances Smith, winner of the Ladies' Amateur Championship in 1949. Daughter of a golf professional and a brave player, she won all the top honours before retiring from the exhausting major golf circuit to bring up her daughter.

Philomena Garvey in action, June 1960: hitting an iron shot from a grassy hill.

A chic champion from Paris, Vicomtesse 'Lally' de Saint Sauveur, winner of the Ladies' Amateur Championship in 1950.

A former dancer, Mrs. Marley Spearman is one of today's successful and stylish players. Marley is a great competitor and practises hard; she never misses her daily practice in the nets at home.

One of the great little lady champions,
Mrs. Jessie Valentine was still winning
twenty five years after scoring her first big success
in winning the Ladies' Amateur Championship in
1937. Slim but wiry and determined,
Jessie was a real golfing machine.

Miss Patty Berg, a great American golfer who made a
successful career as one of the leading women
professionals, went on an exhibition tour of Europe
in 1963. A great 'show girl', her golf clinics are
polished and very instructive. She still plays
occasionally on the Ladies Pro-circuit and although
almost a veteran now she shows the 'new girls' that the
older heroines can still play first-class golf.

The 1937 winner was to become a most amazing evergreen champion. Miss Jessie Anderson, later Mrs. George Valentine of Perth, was twenty two years old when she became champion in 1937. She repeated her Championship success in 1955 and 1958, over a span of twenty one years. She is still a great player, though she no longer appears in Championships.

An Irish Champion. Ireland's most famous woman golfer, Philomena Garvey, won her country's title more than a dozen times. At her twelfth attempt she became British champion at Gleneagles in 1957. With magnificent courage and skill she prevented an all-American final at Harlech in 1960, though she lost to American champion Barbara McIntyre. She reached the final again at Royal Portrush in 1963, but lost to the powerful French girl, Brigitte Varangot.

These two great players, Philomena Garvey and Brigitte Varangot, had battered their way through a storm-tossed Championship. Twenty three year old Brigitte, now France's leading player, was spurred on to the victory by the knowledge that another great French player, Vicomtesse de Saint Sauveur, had won on the same course in 1950, the last occasion on which the Championship was played at Gleneagles.

Another dedicated player is Mrs. Marley Spearman, winner of the 1961 Championship at Carnoustie, who performed the difficult feat of retaining her title the following year, when she beat the English champion, Mrs. Angela Bonallack, in a very exciting final.

Over the Years. In a short time women have come a long way in the world of golf.

At the beginning it would have seemed unbelievable that a woman called Joyce Wethered would reach a standard differing from that of her brother Roger, an Amateur champion, by 'from two to seven strokes according to the course', nor that in the United States women professionals like Mrs. 'Babe' Zaharias, Misses Patty Berg, Louise Suggs and Mickey Wright, would one day play in their own big money tournaments and produce a standard of play differing only from men's in being on a slightly smaller scale of distance, but hardly at all on a lower scale of skill.

The next scene in the drama might well be a full dress test on level terms between representative teams of the world's best players, men and women!

Miss Carol Sorenson of America, British Lady Champion of 1964.

A woman's swing is usually very long, but this must surely be about the limit. Mrs. J. Kendall practices at Westchester Country Club, New York. I find it amazing that anyone can get back to hit the ball from such a back swing.

The
Curtis Cup

The distinction of having staged the first international golf match between Great Britain and the United States belongs to the ladies of the links. It was held at Cromer in 1905 initiated by the American players as a rehearsal-cum-practice for the British Ladies' Championship. This first international between Britain and America was won by the British ladies by six matches to one. Though this was an unofficial international, no advance plans having been made to stage it, its link with the Curtis Cup is very evident. For among the American players in this match were the sisters Margaret and Harriet Curtis, who later donated the trophy which bears their name, and which is played for biennially in America and the British Isles alternately.

The first Curtis Cup match was played in 1932 and since then Britain has won the Cup twice only. They have, however, gained some glory by halving the 1958 match with the Americans on their own territory. The last British Isles victory was at Sandwich in 1956.

The 1964 British Isles Curtis Cup team was selected after the International matches between the four home countries: England, Ireland, Scotland, and Wales. As England retained the International Shield it was natural that the team should be mainly English, the only 'outsider' being the Scottish champion. Ireland was not represented on the team. The leading Irish golfer Philomena Garvey had turned professional earlier in the year, and the Emerald Isle can, at present, produce no player qualified to take her place in these international events.

We lost by $10\frac{1}{2}$ to $7\frac{1}{2}$ points but the match was much more exciting than the score suggests.

Leading the British team at Royal Porthcawl were the top English players of the past several years: Marley Spearman, twice winner of the British Ladies' Open Championship, who added the 1962 title to her list of honours, and Angela Bonallack, English champion of the previous year. There was no British champion to give inspiration to the home side. Marley Spearman had lost her title to French champion Brigitte Varangot in the stormswept Championship of 1963 at Royal County Down in Ireland, and the 1964 Ladies' Open had been won by American Carol Sorensen.

This match was a personal triumph for Marley Spearman, for apart from winning both her foursomes she halved both her singles in which she met the two most powerful and experienced players of the opposing side: American champion Barbara McIntyre, playing in her fourth Curtis Cup match, and Jeanne Gunderson also with three Internationals behind her. Miss Gunderson was the longest hitter in a powerful American team and she outdrove Marley from the tee at every hole, and came to the last hole one up.

Altogether there was much courage shown on both sides, but the Americans appeared to be stronger physically and to have more powers of endurance.

Miss Philomena Garvey, Ireland's greatest woman golfer and now a professional, has won most of golf's top honours. Philomena is a natural sort of player who uses an interlocking grip and is always attacking the ball and the hole.

Two great lady champions: Mrs. Marley Spearman watches Mrs. Frances Smith drive.

Mrs. Angela Bonallack, wife of one of our best British Amateurs, Michael Bonallack, is dressed here for comfort and protection against the English climate. She appears a little displeased with her iron shot.

A champion of today: American Miss Barbara McIntyre, holder of the British and American Ladies' Championships, and Curtis Cup player. This elegant brunette has great concentration.

Golfing around the world

Golf is today an international sport. Some countries still only possess one course, but most countries are dotted with links to cater for the millions to whom the game has become a lifetime hobby.

In Europe interest in the game developed slowly but the beginning of the twentieth century saw a great surge of enthusiasm fanned by the French triumphs in the British Open and Ladies' Championships. A growing number of professional players from Spain, Italy and Western Europe have since maintained the Continental challenge.

Outside of Scotland and England, the oldest golf clubs in the world are the Royal Calcutta Golf Club and the Royal Bombay Golfing Society, both of which date back to the early nineteenth century. By the middle of that century there were as many clubs in India as in England. Calcutta and Bombay were the forerunners of a great number of clubs in the Far East. There was a club in Java twenty years before any course existed in Holland, and golf has been played in Siam, now Thailand, for almost as many years as in the United States, the first Siamese clubhouse being an ancient and very Oriental temple.

China and Japan joined the golfing round in the first years of this century, though the site of the first Japanese course must have eliminated all but the most stout-hearted golfers. It was situated on the summit of Mount Rokko in Kobe. It took about an hour and a half to reach the course in pre-motor days, the journey entailing a rickshaw ride to the foot of the Cascade Valley from where the coolies took over, carrying the players up the mountain. Despite this, or perhaps even because of it, golf flourished in Japan and between the two wars Japanese professionals competed in both British and American events.

Australia, New Zealand, South Africa: by the early eighties golf had been established in every part of the British Commonwealth. Canada anticipated the arrival of the game in the United States by about fifteen years with the formation of the Royal Montreal Club in 1873.

The birth of golf in the United States took place at a dinner party in the home of John Reid at Yonkers, New York, on 14 November, 1888. Reid and his four friends elected themselves as officials of a club which they respectfully called St. Andrews. The first course was a three-hole one in Reid's cow pasture. It increased to six holes when it was moved to a thirty acre pasture and it gained new stature in its third move to an apple orchard on Palisade Avenue. It was a fairly obvious result that these pioneer golfers should from then on be known as the 'Apple Tree Gang'.

They would be astonished to discover the giant they had fathered. For today over five million Americans each play at least twelve rounds of golf a year over almost six thousand courses in the United States. A conservative estimate of the real estate value of existing golf courses and facilities is 2,000,000,000 dollars and the sales of

The most famous Clubhouse in the world: the grey granite home of the Royal and Ancient Golf Club at St. Andrews. This is the mecca which draws golf enthusiasts from all over the world. The tall towered building on the right was formerly the Grand Hotel; now it is a Students' hostel. During the big Championship weeks hotel accommodation is at a premium in the 'Auld Grey Toon'. Considering that St. Andrews hopes to become the permanent home of major championships, I have never been able to understand why the municipality is so lacking in foresight as to allow the hotels to continue to disappear, as they do, yearly.

A view that thrills every golfer: the 18th and 1st fairway of the Old Course at St. Andrews, seen from the upper windows of Rusack's Hotel. This turf has been walked on by millions of golfers in the close on four hundred years that the game has been played on this piece of Scottish coast. The Open Championships are in play and the crowds are marshalled off the course, only being allowed to cross from one side of the fairway to the other between pairings. This turns the course into a golfing arena. With the number of spectators increasing yearly this arrangement has become unsatisfactory as the spectators are too far away from the actual play.

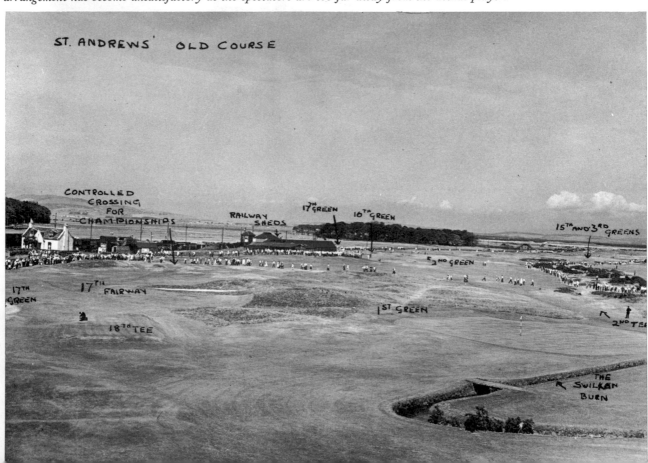

ST. ANDREWS' OLD COURSE

The first tee of the Lundin Links golf club, one of Scotland's seaside links. This course, which is on the very edge of the Firth of Forth, has a fine golfing tradition and the keenest group of members. I like the pathway built on the left to preserve the 1st tee from the excessive wear which would be caused by the hundreds of caddie carts which are pulled round this old links every week.

A picturesque view of the 5th green on the Ailsa Course at the Turnberry Hotel. Situated on the west coast of Scotland, not far from Glasgow, this is a golfing paradise.

Turnberry Hotel from the 18th green of the Ailsa Golf Course.

Heathland golf at its best on a summer's day at Walton Heath with the heather and bracken in full beauty. Today this open heath has reverted to its former image when there were but few trees. Sir William Carr, chairman of the club, believes he should preserve the heritage which his father, a founder member of the club in 1904, left him. Sir Emsley Carr believed a heath should be open and windswept and that the holes should not lie in avenues of trees. His son upholds this opinion. 'Trees are all right for park courses,' says Sir William.

The bungalow-style clubhouse at the Langley Park Golf Club, a lovely park course just a few miles from London, at Beckenham, Kent. This course is still in the most perfect condition. I was professional at the club from 1926 to 1932 and I am a proud Honorary Member of it.

A memory of the autumn of 1945, with the afternoon sun lighting up the stately front of the clubhouse of the Moor Park Golf Club at Rickmansworth, near London. Sheep are still in possession of the course which they took over during the war years. Although the war had ended a few months previous to this the farmers' lease had not yet run out. Before the advent of the lawn mower, sheep were extensively used for cropping the grass on courses. In fact the original bunkers were made by sheep sheltering from the cold sea breezes that swept our coastal links. Nowadays sheep are not popular on golf courses; they dirty the ground, burn the green and make the fairways tufty.

West Hill Golf Club, Surrey: a charming course on beautiful turf in ideal golfing country amid heath, heather and pines. The sort of course one could never tire of playing on.

Beautiful Stoke Poges, a parkland course near London. The swans watch with graceful disdain the progress of a tournament.

A luxury setting for golf on the Florida coast: the famous Boca Raton Hotel and courses, where Sam Snead is professional in the winter season. The building juts out into a famous inland waterway only a few yards off the sea and beach. The entrance to the hotel is a majestic avenue of royal palms. The first hole of the course runs from the rear end of the white path on the left of the photograph. The course lies on pure white sand and it is only necessary to dig a hole to make a bunker; the many bunkers, as can be seen, are very big. The climate is wonderful here, and there is plenty of amusement but it is expensive, as are most American resorts. Fred Perry, our last great Wimbledon tennis champion, was professional tennis coach at this plush club for many years.

This is the scene of the 1964 U.S. Open Championship. The huge building in the background is the Congressional Golf Club, Washington. Subscriptions are, of necessity, very high to maintain such a luxurious building. The 18th hole is the short hole over the lake but to make it easier for officials to control the crowd the courses ended at the testing 17th hole, seen in the foreground, where an arm of the lake lies parallel with the length of the green on the left. This hole became then a 'do or die' finishing hole. Other holes from the club's extra nine holes were fitted into the Championship layout to make up a 7073 yards course.

A view of the famous water hole, the 16th, at the Augusta National Course in Georgia, U.S.A., scene of the annual
120,000 dollar Masters' Tournament. This event attracts such crowds that spectators have to reserve places.
Ten thousand cars are parked there during each day's play and there are special viewing stands and catering facilities
for the crowds. The chairman of the Tournament Committee, Clifford Roberts, always seeking perfection in
his running of this great event, has for some years added copper sulphate crystals to this stretch of water to
enhance its colour, usually a muddy brown. Each hole on the course is named after a flowering shrub or tree and
naturally specimens of each type are to be found growing along the holes somewhere. At one tournament I saw Byron
Nelson, one of golf's all-time greats, strike the flagstick at the water hole with his tee shot, when the hole was cut
just over the small bunker on the left front of the green. The ball flew back into the water and Nelson had to go
back over the lake to play his second shot from there. Really tough luck this, the sort of luck that cannot be
eliminated from golf, but which ruins a golfer's chance of winning by punishing him for being too accurate.

Leaning palms lend atmosphere to the luxurious
Indian Creek Country Club at Miami Beach, Florida,
one of the greatest clubs and courses in the
whole of Florida. Meals served in the restaurant here
are quite fantastic, certainly among the finest I have
had anywhere. Members use no cash at this club. They
sign vouchers for all their outgoings: green fees,
guests, caddies, meals, and purchases in the pro's shop.
Accounts are settled monthly and the annual deficit
in the operation of the club, if any, is divided
equally between the members for payment.

Golf is a popular feature on American television. They use a 'Cherry Picker' to film the game. From this high nest a camera can get bird's eye shots of the flat courses, which certainly makes the film exciting.

A comprehensive guide to the Inagawa Course. There are many driving ranges being built, in fact there are already far more golfers than can find room to play on the three hundred existing courses. The Japanese is a glutton for practice and enjoys playing on the driving ranges, patiently and perseveringly trying to improve his technique. To date there are few good players there but the victory of the two Japanese professionals over Snead and Demaret, U.S.A. in the 1956 Canada Cup Match has given fresh impetus to the growth of the game in Japan.

The famous clubhouse of the Mar del Plata Golf Club in the Argentine, where I spent the winter of 1929–30 teaching. This popular seaside course runs on a hillside overlooking the beach and the port. The clubhouse is a fine building, beautifully appointed, with a restaurant and locker rooms equal to the best in the world.

The 1st hole from the tee at the Naruo Golf Club in Japan.

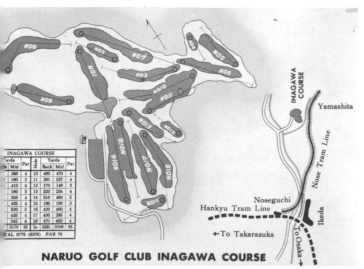

INAGAWA COURSE						
	Yards	Par	Hole	Yards	Par
	Back	Mid			Back	Mid
	360	4	10	480	470	4
	160	3	11	391	337	4
	410	4	12	170	148	3
	160	3	13	320	256	4
	355	4	14	510	460	5
	425	4	15	190	190	3
	520	5	16	420	400	4
	435	4	17	430	395	4
	345	4	18	470	450	4
	3170	35	In	3381	3106	35
TOTAL 6775 (6276) PAR 70						

NARUO GOLF CLUB INAGAWA COURSE

golf balls alone in recent years has exceeded 30,000,000 dollars.

Where Nations Meet. Matches between the British Isles and other countries extend golfing hands of friendship across the seas of the world. Apart from the Walker, Ryder and Curtis Cups, there are many Continental matches and all the Championships have some British entrants.

The Ladies' Commonwealth Tournament, instituted at St. Andrews during the Royal and Ancient Bicentenary Celebrations of 1954, is played every four years in each of the Commonwealth countries successively. Lady golfers had their first match at St. Andrews in 1959 and the venue in 1963 was New Zealand.

The annual competition for the Canada Cup in which two professional players from each country compete, began in 1953 and the trophy was won for the first time by Argentina, represented by Antonio Cerda and Roberto de Vicenzo. Eire won when represented by Harry Bradshaw and Christie O'Connor. America won in 1956 with the partnership of Ben Hogan and Sam Snead, and

Japan the following year via K. Ono and T. Nakamura, the latter also winning the individual prize with 274. The venues are world-wide and have included Tokyo, Mexico City, Ireland and Australia. The trophy was competed for in December 1964 at Hawaii when Arnold Palmer and Jack Nicklaus for U.S.A. won the team prize and Nicklaus the individual prize.

Four players from each country compete in the well-established team Championship for the Eisenhower World Cup, another coveted international trophy which was won by Great Britain and Ireland for the first time in 1964 when they beat Canada into second place at Olgiata near Rome.

The year 1964 saw the debut of the World Matchplay Tournament at Wentworth in October. This is a very select field of eight players chosen by the organisers from all over the world and the first famous contestants were Arnold Palmer, Gary Player, Jack Nicklaus, Ken Vertini, Bruce Devlin, Tony Lema, Neil Coles and Peter Butler. The first prize of £5,000 was won by American Arnold Palmer who beat Britain's Neil Coles in the final by 2 and 1.

I concentrate on my putt on the first green of the Hotel du Golf at Deauville, which is situated right by the first tee, in the very centre of the course. This hotel was built in 1929 by Monsieur Francois Andre when he was head of the Deauville Casino and the hotel chain. He realised that golf would attract the right clientele to enhance his business ventures and he was proved right. Today the course is open all the year round, previously it was just a short season summer course. Now with a new Autoroute to Normandy being pushed farther and farther out of Paris, Deauville will soon be just a couple of hours run for the teeming millions of the French capital.

Reconstructed from old farm buildings, the clubhouse of the St. Nom la Bretèche Golf Club near Paris cost around £400,000 and is one of the most beautifully appointed clubhouses in Europe. The first tees of the thirty six holes of golf at the club are on the left of the picture, some two hundred yards from the locker rooms.

The golf course on Mont Agel, three thousand feet up behind the Principality of Monaco, which I rebuilt in 1945 and 1946. It is a short hilly course, fun to play but tough to walk.

A golf scene in Germany: the German Open Championship at Frankfort on Main. A fine test of golf here is a dense pine forest. I do not remember why the flag is so much on the front of the green, especially as the green is big. This is unusual, but I feel there must have been a good reason.

A pause during a round with John Jay Hopkins (centre), founder of the Canada Cup, and Harry Weetman.

Ben Hogan in action at Wentworth during the Canada Cup 1954.

A Triumph for France. Another welcome addition to the international round is the Women's World Cup, sponsored by the Ladies' Golfing Unions of the World. The idea for this event originated from the Federation Française de Golf only a year before it was played. The original suggestion was for a match between France and America but the United States Golf Association amplified this by suggesting a World Team Championship to be held biennially. Most of the work involved in the organising of the event was done by Vicomtesse de Saint Sauveur, France's most celebrated woman golfer, who won the French Championship ten times in all and our Ladies' Open and has represented her country for over twenty years in international events.

Flags of twenty five nations were flying on the Saint-Germain course when the first of the series was held in Paris in October 1964. There were fifty hostesses, who appeared to be multilingual, and as the starter announced each player he gave brief details of her playing career. Each country was represented by a team of three players, England's first team being Marley Spearman, Ruth Porter and Bridget Jackson. The two best scores of the teams of three counted, so that a player could come into the picture on any of the four days of the event.

The organisation was perfect to the last detail and it seemed only fitting that France, who had proposed the Championship, should win this epoch-making world event. They did so with an aggregate of 588, the United States finishing with 589, England with 591 and Canada with 606.

The bright particular star of the French side was nineteen year old Catherine Lacoste who opened with 72 and was followed by Brigitte Varangot with 75 to give France the lead on the first day with 147.

America finished the first day a stroke behind France with 148, with Barbara Fay White's score of 73 and Carol Sorensen, who had just won the British Championship, producing 75.

On the second day Catherine Lacoste had 71 and Claudine Cros 75, which put them two strokes ahead of the United States and four ahead of England.

The United States took the lead on the third day with 440; Carol Sorensen with 72 and Barbara Fay White with 73. France was a stroke behind with 441.

The final day was tense indeed. Brigitte Varangot had 77 and Claudine Cros 74, while for America Carol Sorensen had 73 and Barbara Fay White 76. All depended on the third player of each team. Catherine Lacoste finished first with 73, brilliant as ever except for a five at a short hole. American champion Barbara McIntyre, who had not been on top form, had the chance to produce the winning score. She needed a final four. She bunkered her second shot and her third shot and in the end she just failed to hole an eight-yard putt to tie.

The nations competing in the order in which they finished were: France, United States, England, Canada,

Australia, New Zealand, Sweden, Germany, Scotland, Mexico, Belgium, South Africa, Wales, Ireland, Italy, Holland, Philippines, Chile, Japan, Argentina, Spain, Portugal, Denmark, Bermuda, and Austria.
The next Women's Championship will probably be played in Mexico in 1966.

A great French player who shone in the first Women's World Cup in 1964, nineteen year old Catherine Lacoste.

Carol Sorenson, U.S.A., watches the finish of her drive during the 1964 World Championship in Paris. Seated at the side is Catherine Lacoste of France.

H.R.H. The Duke of Windsor watches the World Team Championship at St. Germain near Paris.

What could better illustrate 'golfing round the world' than this rolling golf course on the high seas: putting on the S.S. Andes *en route to South America. This shipboard golf is possible with the steady trade winds which just rock the ship very slowly so that it is possible to judge this movement and putt quite well. I used to watch the shadow carefully and time my stroke.*

Short courses
and driving range

*The latest in driving ranges: a double-tier
construction illuminated for night play. Dozens of
players can practice here in all weathers. America is
dotted with these ranges and they are now growing in
popularity in England.*

One of the developments which is steadily increasing in
popularity and which has, I think, a definite position in
the future of the game is the form of training available
at the short courses and driving ranges.

There are over one thousand five hundred of these
training arenas in America, and many of them stay open
till the small hours of the morning, so that night workers
can drop in for some fresh air and practice after their
work shift.

For many years the British public repudiated these
ranges; now they are springing up, and operating most
successfully, all over our islands. If well located I am
convinced they can be a most profitable undertaking.

A first-class range can be constructed on a dozen acres.
They can be simple affairs, tee mats on open ground, or
more elaborate affairs with illuminated double-tier
buildings with plush car parks, restaurants and bars.

The one snag to the successful operation of these ranges
is the propensity of clients to steal the golf balls. Painting
the balls yellow or encircling them with red stripes is
apparently no deterrent; they will still be stolen for use
on golf courses. This is quite shameful of course and it is
rather hard to understand why people who would never
contemplate stealing money will nevertheless steal
property in this way.

*A rooftop driving range of the mid-twenties.
Harry Vardon and James Braid watch American-Scot
Macdonald Smith drive a ball into a huge netted
area in Piccadilly.*

*The covered shed is an essential part of a club's
practice ground. It should be heated with a stove for
cold winter days and be built high for brightness and to
allow for free swinging. Here I am coaching Walker Cup
star Harry Bentley in one of the three solid sheds
at the Ashridge Club, Herts, built in 1937. Some
professionals have portable sheds in transparent
material for all weather teaching.*

*These well-designed covered sheds at the Deauville
Golf Club in France were built in 1964 and, of course,
they face on to the practice ground. The roof is of
transparent material and the rear part of the
construction is closed in to house the hundreds of
bag trolleys in use during the big season.*

*This tricycle golf ball shield for the girl 'picker
upper' at the Deauville driving range in France
was constructed by the local bicycle dealer. The wire
baskets in which the balls are hired out are hung
round the cage and when there are a lot of full
baskets this contraption can become very heavy to push.*

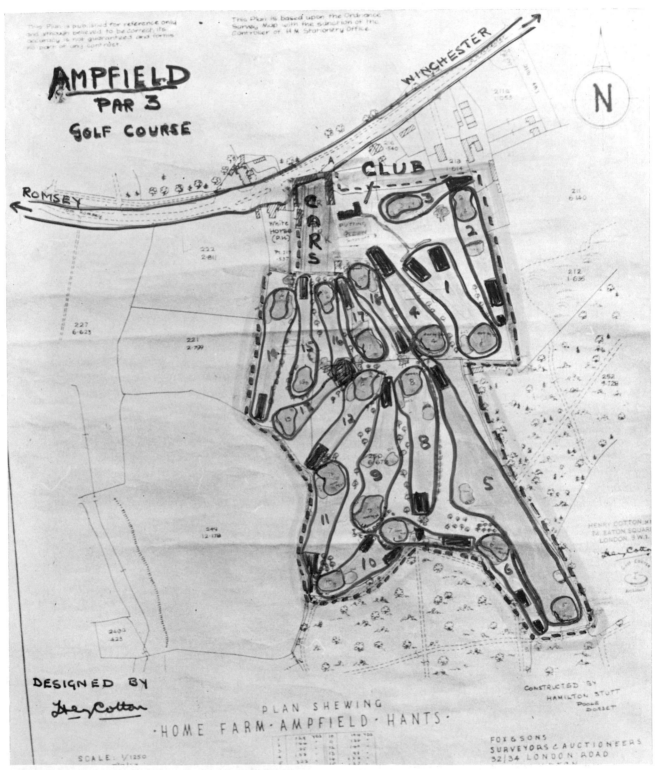

The par 3 course at Ampfield which I designed. One par 3 hole makes this little course of par 3 holes different and exciting to play. Built on twenty two acres only, a round can be played in an hour; on a big course it sometimes takes well over three hours. This project has a fine car park, a fully-equipped clubhouse, a putting green, a resident professional and properly built-up greens.

This driving range at Finchley, North London, is built on the American pattern with automatic tees. It can accommodate forty eight players and is lighted for evening play.

The golf driving range human ball 'picker upper' of the Milan Golf Club, Monza, Italy. This is his own idea of protection and it leaves him fairly vulnerable to a 'frontal' attack. He admits to getting a few hits but he has developed an instinct for keeping his back to the line of fire. With his home-made ball scoop he handles thousands of balls on a busy day.

A necessary part of the successful driving range, the ball 'picker upper'. This great labour saver is pushed before a tractor; obviously if towed the tractor wheels would bury the balls.

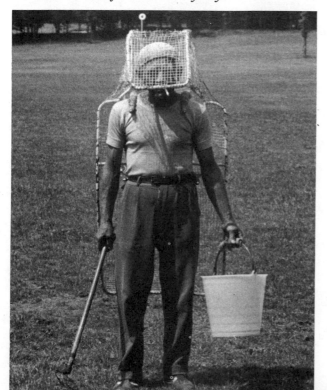

Kings of
the courses

The rules, the clubs, the competitions, the courses: all of these have played an important part in the development of the game. But our golfing heritage, the essence and spirit of the game we know and love, was bequeathed to us by the players and the officials who nourished the game from its puny infancy to the triumphant independence of today.

There is a certain magic in the names of those illustrious players who, by their achievements and their personalities, enhanced the stature of the game. John Ball, James Braid, Harry Vardon and J. H. Taylor, Walter Hagen, Harold Hilton, Robert Tyre Jones: these and many others have a place in all golfing reminiscences.

Golf's 'great ones' deserve to be remembered by our younger generation of players, for it is unlikely that the modern player will ever see or read about any greater or more sterling players. They played when golf was far more difficult than it is today, when steel shafts were unknown and golf balls were not made to fly great distances. Arnold Palmer, after a recent test with a set of hickory-shafted clubs, reckoned they were six shots per round more difficult to use. They did not have the clubs to fit the distances to within ten yards; they had to hit the ball with all the strength the wooden-shafted clubs would stand, and they used cleeks, clubs that needed great skill, and with them they played all manner of shots, including the spared shot to the green which rolled the ball up to the hole. They also negotiated the stymie, now a forgotten art. They were great golfers, all of them. And our Triumvirate, Vardon, Taylor and Braid, Robert Tyre Jones and Walter Hagen were perhaps the greatest of the great ones.

The Strong Silent Golfer. Many champions use golf to live. James Braid, one of my heroes, lived for golf. He just loved the game, finding equal joy in competing in a Championship or merely playing a few holes with a pupil around his beloved Walton Heath, carrying five clubs with him in a tiny canvas bag.

He was one of the golfing heroes of yesteryear. Yet when, as a young man, he left his native Scotland to come south to be an instructor he undertook one of his longest journeys! He was the least-travelled of the big names of his day. With Harry Vardon and J. H. Taylor he dominated the game during the twenty years before the First World War, and he was the first of this great Triumvirate to win the Open Championship five times. His Championship career was the briefest of the three but the most brilliant.

A plasterer in Fife, Braid took up golf in his spare time and from the beginning he lashed the ball with what writer Bernard Darwin called 'a divine fury'.

Even in the days when I was first privileged to play with him – he must have been fifty six years old then – he still attacked the ball with a refreshing vigour.

He was a tall powerful man, strong and silent would describe him well, and how right was the person who said 'Nobody could be as wise as James Braid looked.' He rarely spoke in public; indeed there were few occasions on which he could be persuaded to stand up and say even a few words.

He was professional at Walton Heath for forty six years, until he died at the age of eighty in 1950, and he held an honorary membership of the club for twenty five of those years.

What always amazed me about Jimmy was the way he could beat his age. He started doing this at sixty six, and never stopped. In fact he looked forward to going round on 6 February, his birthday, to see if he could begin his new year with a new record.

I like the story of the American visitor to Walton Heath who asked the club secretary to find him a partner. Braid was suggested and the name clearly did not register with the visitor. They played and Jimmy, almost unbeatable at home, gave him the 'works', much to the American's surprise.

When asked how he liked the course the visitor said he had enjoyed it very much, but he was amazed at the performance of the old man from the tin hut. 'He must have been some shooter in his young days,' he added.

Jimmy was technically a sound golfer and possessed a wonderful temperament for the game. I used to play with him regularly, for I too love Walton Heath, and he was always referee on the many occasions the *News of the World* sponsored big money matches in which I was invited to take part.

Right to the end he got a great kick from being among golfers and listening to their stories, as he sat sipping his favourite drink of port after lunch.

Though for years he had been financially independent, he loved to play and teach golf and to spend an evening at the village club with his friends.

There is a wonderful painting of this great man in the clubhouse at Walton Heath, the club which he served faithfully for so many years.

The Incomparable Bobby Jones. Every succeeding generation, while glorying like youth in its own powers, yet casts an eye back on the earlier generations, secretly wondering just how good they were. Bobby Jones, now alas a cripple though still only sixty three years of age, can compare and discuss the present and the past.

Bobby – he will always be that to us, though he prefers to be called Bob – still holds the greatest record of all time. Crammed into a short space of eight years he did more than others have achieved in a lifetime before he retired at the age of twenty eight.

He entered in twenty one major events on both sides of the Atlantic and won thirteen of them.

It is easier to play golf, it seems, every year; this is good, adding to the enjoyment of the game. But young players should be reminded that in Jones' days, and long before that, there was more rough on the courses and the greens were not soaked daily. Those who have known big golf

Dressed in his Clan tartan, James Braid poses in a studio in Ballater, Scotland.

when courses were like ice-rinks and demanded a touch 'like a mother's kiss' will realise what a continuous strain it was on the nerves to keep the ball under control and collect fours on the card.

When asked about his health today Bob Jones replies 'About the same,' for an injured vertebra at the top of the spine has caused an increasing atrophy and pain in his arms and legs. Two operations some years back have failed to correct the trouble, but he gets about with the aid of two sticks stamped 'Robert T. Jones, Jnr'; this was stamped on his winning golf clubs years ago when they were hand-forged in Scotland.

Bob Jones considers that steel shafts have greatly helped scoring; the light shaft and better weight distribution, more in the head, plus the elimination of torsion, are big features. Players today can hit full out; there is no need to spare the club. Players are driving further because of the shaft, not so much because of the better ball, though the modern ball carries farther than the balls of years ago, which were softer and rolled.

When Jones was at his peak, the tradition that every player had one bad round persisted; today you need all good rounds. Today the top players play the whole year round in competitive golf; in Jones' day six events a year was his maximum. I found that Bob never considered golf to be the most important thing in his life; he always had other interests, but he reasoned as a lawyer 'If I had decided I was going to play a tournament every week for the rest of my life, maybe I could have prepared myself for it.' He meant, fate permitting.

Walter Hagen lost his enthusiasm for tournaments and travelling around before he was forty, and whilst he had never lost the idea that he had to play to live, he had no incentive for competitive golf. This Jones considers a decisive factor in a golfer's career.

I talked with him on the question of the strain in big golf, because every great golfer has experienced this. Jones' reply was that he always loved golf, always loved playing (I played with him in 1948 at Augusta National Golf Club, which must have been the last year he was

An interesting picture of Walter Hagen, U.S.A., playing a left-handed shot from beneath a tree, watched by a small crowd of enthralled spectators. This picture was taken during an exhibition tour in the Far East, where golf is now booming. Hagen and his partner, Joe Kirkwood, made many successful and profitable world tours, but Hagen never tried to save money: he wanted to live and see the world. 'I have had a good time,' he used to tell me, 'and they can't take that away!' Now a monumental figure, living for his shooting and fishing, he has not touched a club for years. Yet 'the Haig' or 'Sir Walter', to the press, remains one of the world's most honoured heroes of the game.

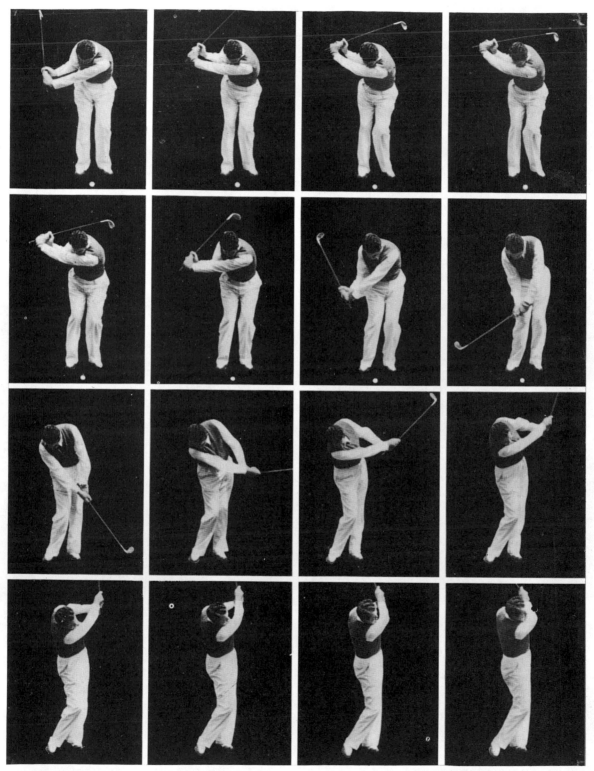

Ralph Guldhall, a repeat winner of the U.S. Open in 1937 and 1938, a rare achievement.
He had a very upright action and was a most accurate player. Notice the curious right-hand action.
Like Abe Mitchell, Alfred Perry, the Whitcombes, Bobby Locke and Dai Rees he allowed the club shaft
to slide about in the right palm. It is rather curious that all these players are, or were, most
accurate in their best playing days.

Reginald (Reggie) Whitcombe, youngest brother of the
famous golfing family and winner of the Open
Championship in 1938. He was a more daring player
than his two elder brothers though he played naturally,
as they did. The ball was there to be hit, and he got on
with it with the minimum of fuss.

Charles Whitcombe in action, with the ball heading
directly for the flag and his eyes still glued to
the spot where the ball had been. He was one of the
straightest players I ever saw or played against.
Using thick rubber grips he had the simplest set of
actions, very upright indeed.

Ernest Whitcombe, Ryder Cup player and a popular professional at the Meyrick Park Club in Bournemouth. The three Whitcombe brothers, of whom Ernest was the eldest, were all fine natural golfers and very successful and prominent in British golf for nearly twenty years. They all used the interlocking grip.

able to play properly), never got sick of the game, but got fed up with the 'damn punishment' of big events.

Bob repeats with relish the story of Sam Snead, who is still bursting to win the U.S. Open, a title which has eluded him. Sam once asked him 'which one of the championships that you won did you want to win most?' 'Sam,' replied Bob, 'it was always the one I was playing at the time, and if I had not felt that way I would not have won any.'

The good old chestnut of the interviewing reporter comes next. 'Do you think the best golfers of your day were as good as the best golfers of the present day?' Knowing the answer to his chestnut by heart, Bob replies with his soft Georgian drawl and gentle courtesy, giving Ben Hogan a break: 'All you can beat are the people that are around at the same time as you are – you cannot beat the ones that came before or the ones that came after. How can you compare Vardon with me, or Hogan or Tom Morris?' Ben Hogan says a man who is capable of being a champion in one era could be a champion in another.

The story of Sergeant York, a hero of the First World War, reminds him, in a back-handed way, of his reply. For the Sergeant, when asked on his return how he had made out in the war said: 'Well, I killed more of them than they did of me.'

On the subject of so much waste of time on the courses today, Bob thinks that many players take a lot of time on the green to tranquillise their breathing. He found that the exertion of pushing a way through the crowd in his day was exhausting and he needed time to get composed. But many young players today waste a lot of time studying the shots, trying to take into consideration a lot more things than are necessary.

Bob thinks the Professional Golfers' Association of the United States did right to change their only Matchplay event to a medal play one, as the public like medal events. So much more to see, and the customer is always right. There is no professional matchplay event today, even Television matches are by medal play. He said he might have retired even if he had not won the 'Grand Slam' in 1930: the Amateur Championships of U.S.A. and Great Britain and the two Opens of these two countries. But winning gave him the opportunity to make some films and to join the board of Spaldings, on which he has sat since 1931; he is now a Vice-President. He has also some interests in Coca-Cola bottling plants in America and overseas; these are still considered little 'gold mines'.

Despite the fact that in 1931 he forfeited his amateur status, we in the profession and millions of other golfers still consider him an amateur in the general noble way. I do not think the pros of his generation resented him winning; they were human enough to have disliked it, but he was so gracious and gentlemanly that no one could help liking him. I do not think, as the game has gone, there can ever be another quite as outstanding.

On being asked by me how he considers he would have fared in the game today he made a reply which I think is typical of the great man. 'I would rather someone else speculate about that, but I have not seen anything around that would discourage me from trying.'

Bob attends the annual Master's Tournament at Augusta, Georgia. He is president of the club and has a lovely colonial-style cottage near the 10th tee, but he can only follow the golf if driven round in an electric buggy; even then he selects moments when there is a crowd, so that he can pass unnoticed, he hates sympathy. I have not seen him for over seven years now, but the vivid impression he left with me makes it seem like yesterday.

The 'Haig'. Walter C. Hagen, showman and personality, was America's first real golfing 'great'.

A character who became almost a legend and a player who romped to victory through the sheer impetuosity of his attack, Hagen won about seventy five Tournaments and Championships during his brilliant career, including the American Open twice and the P.G.A. Championship four times in succession.

The height of Hagen's ambition was to win the British Open and he won it four times.

The man who taught the world how to putt was Walter Hagen; he was the wizard of the niblick and the putter. He revelled in hand-to-hand combat, overwhelming his opponent by his vigour and enthusiasm.

He was a born matchwinner, cool and imperturbable. In one big tournament as he was studying the line of a putt a dog snapped up the ball and made off with it. The spot was marked and when the ball had been recovered Hagen duly holed the putt. When a friend exclaimed afterwards how relieved he had been that Hagen had not been put off his form by the incident Hagen was sur-

I share an electric golf buggy with Bobby Jones at Augusta in 1957.

Sam Snead driving at St. Andrews in 1946, when he won the Open. He has never won the U.S. Open in twenty five tries, which is curious considering that he has won over one hundred major events, all over the world when his play has delighted millions. 'Slamming' Sam possesses one of the most powerful and fluent swings in golf, due to his physique and a double-jointed left wrist.

Sam Snead, 1962 version, as he practises at Troon. A little thicker in the body, but the firm grip and fine swing are still in evidence, also the perfect balance, always the sign of a great player.

In his favourite black beret, Norman Von Nida, the little Australian who came to Britain soon after the war and collected a lot of prize money, plays a pitch shot before a Southport crowd in 1947. He was a fine recovery player and a fine putter.

Harry Bradshaw, a jovial Irishman whose round the body scything motion swing and velvet putting touch gave him many high honours in golf for a long period after the Second World War. Here he is putting, his head still down with the ball well on the way. He tied with Bobby Locke for the Open in 1949 but he lost the play off. He had bad luck when his ball finished in a broken bottle, out of which he could have had a free lift. But he played the ball and it took him an extra shot to reach the green. This incident cost him the title.

A study in concentration: Ben Hogan, one of the greatest, stands with head still down while the ball is well on its way.

A. D. 'Bobby' Locke, another top amateur who turned professional after great success as a young amateur. He won four Open Championships, using his old hickory-shafted putter which he is seen using here. He never attacked the hole badly, his putts were delicately judged so that they fell into the hole, rarely striking the back lip. He continued to play good golf until he was involved in an accident in which his car was struck on an unguarded level crossing in South Africa; since then his eyesight has been failing.

Frank Jowle watches Roberto de Vicenzo of the Argentine driving. Vicenzo, one of the game's longest hitters, has only failed to win all the very top honours because of a slight weakness on the greens and perhaps because of his Latin temperament. A former caddie from Palermo in Buenos Aires he has done very well from the game; in 1964 he won seven events in different parts of the world.

A gallery of champions at the famous Masters' Tournament at Augusta, Georgia, in 1957. Left to right: Cary Middlecoff, U.S. Open; Byron Nelson, U.S. Open; Henry Cotton, British Open; Ken Venturi, U.S. Open, and Harvie Ward, British and U.S. Amateur. Byron Nelson was one of the most accurate strikers of a ball ever, and he dominated the American Tournament scene with relentlessly faultless play for some years. He could play all the shots and he made the game look easy, even if his double knee 'duck' going through the ball was original at the time. Many power players play this way today. Ken Venturi was still an Amateur when this photograph was taken. He won the U.S. Open in a spectacular fashion in 1964 and got himself into the very big money overnight after a lean spell of over two years.

Bernard Hunt, one of the top playing professionals of the past decade. Still in his early thirties, Hunt was leading money winner in 1963 and he played in the 1953 Ryder Cup team at Wentworth when we lost by the barest margin. Seated cross-legged among the spectators is film star Richard Todd.

Peter Thomson from Australia, a complete golfer if ever there was one. His swing is simple and strong and he was a wonderful temperament with an iron nerve. He favours the left wrist in line with the forearm act, club face almost fully closed. Not yet thirty years old, Thomson's golfing potential is enormous, for he never wastes a minute and speeds from one tournament to the next by air.

Cary Middlecoff, a double winner of the U.S. Open, and a wonderful competitor. Not a stylist, I have often noticed that his long rangey body makes a neat swing difficult. Here he is finishing a drive; only a contortionist could get into this position. It puts a real strain on his back, which now and then, not surprisingly, gives him trouble. He has twisted his body violently from his ankle to his neck. Cary trained as a dentist and switched to golf when, as an amateur, he found that he was 'pretty good'. The pros affectionately call him 'Doc'.

'You drive for show, you putt for dough' and here Harry Weetman shows just how it is done.

Ken Venturi, one of the top stars in American golf
and a fine swinger of the club. He left the Amateur
ranks in 1957 and had great success as a professional,
then came a slump in his game and his confidence went.
When he had just reached the point of giving up
professional golf he won the U.S. Open in 1964; now he
is on top of the wave again. Venturi considers that
the Open win will be worth over £50,000 to him the
first year. This is real money!

David Thomas, a power player, one of the longest and
straightest drivers of a golf ball in the world.
This six foot four inch giant is quite able to play
the short game as well as he does his long shots but
he has a dread of the little pitch shot.

Julius Boros, of Hungarian extraction, winner of the
U.S. Open in 1952 and 1963, is a reliable golfer with a
phlegmatic temperament and a lazy swing. Boros has
never played golf to the point of being weary of the
game; he just plays when he feels like it.

Christy O'Connor from Dublin, a great natural golfer
with a loose wristy swing. He has not yet won all the
game's top honours, but he is a consistent big
tournament winner. He took over the top place in Irish
golf from Daly and Harry Bradshaw. He is seen here
driving on the Ailsa Course at Turnberry.

prised. 'Why should I be upset?' he asked. 'It was still the same putt, wasn't it?'

Hagen established further claim to a place in golf's gallery of fame by being largely responsible for the change in the status of professional golfers. In an inoffensive, even endearing, way he demanded and got respect for himself and his fellow-professionals.

There are stories told of how 'The Haig', one of his nicknames, would hire a Rolls-Royce while in England and on arrival at the course he would have his hired chauffeur set up a picnic champagne lunch in front of the clubhouse, entry to which was barred at the time to professionals, for class reasons.

Hagen was always late on the tee. He excused his lateness by explaining that his philosophy was not to rush through life but 'to stop and smell the flowers en route'. I always like his other favourite expression, 'I have had a good time and they can't take that away'. So many of us keep putting off pleasures we can take today, waiting for tomorrow, and sometimes the morrows never come.

Jack Nicklaus plays a successful sand shot recovery: notice his extended follow through and knee action. Nicknamed the 'Golden Bear', this very powerful blond player regularly wins long driving competitions with drives of well over three hundred yards. In his brief three years as a professional he has become second only to Arnold Palmer in the world of golf.

The Champions do look at the ball! Arnold Palmer clearly has his head well down with the ball well on the way.

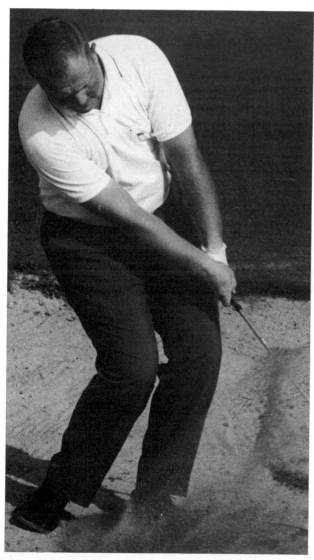

Golf's future hopes

Britain is not rich in young world-beating class golfing talent, but efforts are now being made to produce young champions in sponsored training schemes.

I think Neil Coles heads the list of our coming players, though after his 1964 performance it might be more accurate to say that he has already arrived. He won more money than any other home player during the season, winding up by pocketing £3,000 for his three days' work at Wentworth in the World Championship and ending with £7,400 in official money, he is a 'five figure man'. Coles is one of the most courageous golfers in the country. Nothing daunts him; he is calm and collected, meeting the most renowned opponent with the same assurance he would a friend in a club friendly game. This attitude is disconcerting, to say the least of it, to the stars of the golfing firmament. It was an unusual experience for Arnold Palmer when he met Coles at the World Championship, for this golfing great is accustomed to people metaphorically shaking in their shoes when they meet him on the first tee. But Coles remained unawed and Palmer found himself two down to the British player at the half-way stage. He would have been three down after four holes of the final round if Coles had holed a short but curly downhill putt on the 22nd green in the thirty six holes final. That was where Coles let the greatest golfing draw in the world off the hook, and Palmer seized his chances from there on to become World Champion by a narrow margin of two and one.

But he was deeply impressed with the Britisher's play and said afterwards with a crooked grin 'I don't want to meet Coles again'. Palmer is one of the world's greatest putters, taking command of the greens on the homeward run, while Coles holed nothing of more than a yard. But that is how it goes.

At the 1964 *News of the World* Matchplay Championship at Walton Heath, Coles was considered the winner from the first match.

George Will learned his golf at St. Andrews, where he was born. Having decided to make golf his career he came south to Walton Heath where his boss, Henry Busson, recognised his worth and promoted him to Chief Playing Assistant, now he is professional at the Sundridge Park Golf Club, Bromley, Kent, where he succeeded Alfred Padgham. He has yet to win a major tournament, but he has been well in the running in a number of them. In 1964 he gained valuable experience by playing in the American winter circuit where he was observed by Arnold Palmer who considered that Will was a fine young player in the making.

Brian Huggett and Malcolm Gregson are both promising players. Gregson, in his very early twenties, looks like hitting the high spots before long. He is a Golf Foundation product, having been introduced to golf through class at his school. He has a fine temperament and what I like most about him is that he tries and is not afraid to admit it!

Thirty one year old Neil Coles,
winner of the News of the World *Matchplay*
Championship at Walton Heath in 1964.

George Will, a promising young professional,
playing at Turnberry, a beautiful course on the
western sea coast of Scotland.

Brian Huggett, a determined young Welsh professional.

Malcolm Gregson putting, index finger
extended down the shaft.

Introduced to golf through classes at his school, Malcolm Gregson looks like hitting the high spots before long.

A successful and determined player, five foot two amateur 'Sandy' Saddler gives every shot all he has got.

Son of a professional, Ronnie Shade is one of the finest amateur golfers of the day.

Harold Henning, professional from South Africa. A real trier, he climbed back on top of his game in 1964 after two lean years.

Ronnie Shade is among the best of Britain's young amateurs. He won the Scottish Amateur Championship in 1964 for the second time in succession. In the final he was six under fours for the twenty nine holes he needed to play.

A. C. 'Sandy' Saddler, another Scot, is a 'wee' fellow, with a fine golf game and a big heart. He hurls his frame, five feet two inches and eight stone, at the ball and is great fun to watch.

Pencil-slim Harold Henning is one of the finest and most industrious professional golfers that South Africa has produced, and is highly esteemed by the great Bobby Locke. A perfectionist, he pulled his excellent drive to pieces to see if he could improve on it, but he didn't seem able to put all the pieces back and this gave him two very lean years. He had a great heartener, however, in 1963, when he won £10,000 for a hole-in-one in the Esso Tournament at Moor Park. From then on he started climbing up again to his place on the ladder of fame and 1964 was again a good year for him.

Coby Lagrange, a sturdy determined young South African, is about the same age as Gregson but he has got a jump ahead of the British player with some fine wins in the best company. This religious young golfer is the very epitome of determination and concentration; he must surely take over from Gary Player, who in his turn took over from Locke.

Alex Caygill from Yorkshire is already an established player at twenty four years. But the grind of competitive golf, fifty rounds in 1964, gave him a perforated ulcer which needed surgical treatment. He has great power and determination and should soon be taking over from the old gang; he will improve a lot yet. In 1963 he won my 'Rookie Prize' for the best young player of the year.

Another player with a bright future is Lionel Platts who gave up his club job to try the tournament circuit. In his first year he finished in seventh place and won nearly £3,000 in prize money. A powerful round-shouldered athletic man, Platts has shown already that he is not afraid to win. He scored his first notable success in the '7 club' Braemar Tournament on the difficult Carnoustie course.

Alex Caygill from Yorkshire, already an established tournament player at the age of twenty four.

Lionel Platts, who finished seventh in the Order of Merit 1964.

Nancy, Lady Astor, took a keen interest in golf and was, for a number of years, President of the Ladies' Golf Union.

All the world plays golf

Kings and commoners, politicians and entertainers, churchmen and men of commerce: all the world plays golf. They bring to it varying degrees of enthusiasm and skill and from it they derive relaxation and excitement in immeasurable abundance.

Most of the world's statesmen have sought their relaxation in golf. General Eisenhower, a great enthusiast, had a golf museum in Washington which he showed to favoured visitors. Former British Prime Minister Harold Macmillan played golf whenever possible and so did the late President of the United States, Jack Kennedy. Harold Wilson, the Prime Minister who followed Sir Alec Douglas-Home, is an enthusiastic golfer when time permits.

Famous sportsmen almost always list golf among their favourite sports. Perhaps the greatest all-round sportsman of all was Lord Brabazon of Tara, who died in 1964. Aeroplanes, cars, skis were among his sporting equipment, but there was nothing he liked better than a round of golf. He has been known to fly his own plane to the course to watch a Championship.

Stars of the entertainment world usually relax on a golf course. American show business and golfing personalities include Danny Kaye and, of course, the famous golfing pair, Bob Hope and Bing Crosby. Television's Cliff Michelmore and Eric Sykes, cartoonist Roy Ullyett, billiard and snooker ace Joe Davis are among the British enthusiasts, while some of our stage stars partner golfing professionals in the annual Bowmaker Tournament at Sunningdale and try, with great enthusiasm, to assist their partners to a share of the £3,000 prize money. Among the famous women who loved the game was the late Nancy, Lady Astor. She was, for a number of years, President of the Ladies' Golf Union and she enlivened the meetings with her quick wit and fund of entertaining anecdotes.

A meeting with ex-Prime Minister Harold Macmillan and Lady Dorothy at Nairn course on the North East coast of Scotland, one of Mr. Macmillan's favourite courses.

The late Sir Winston Churchill golfing at Cannes.

Ex-U.S.A. President Dwight Eisenhower.

147

War hero Group Captain Douglas Bader plays golf regularly on his pair of tin legs. At one time he had a single figure handicap. He never feels the cold and is seen here playing in a short-sleeved shirt in midwinter.

Henry Longhurst, radio and television commentator and one of the game's great scribes. A brilliant speaker, Henry was a fine golfer himself in his young days.

Vernon Sangster, Mr. Vernon of the famous Liverpool football pools, is a really keen golfer. He always bandages his right wrist before play because of damaged tendons; the support from the bandage helps him to use his hand to better advantage.

Bettina, the well-known former model and fiancée of the late Aly Khan, golfing at Deauville. I gave Bettina a number of lessons but although she had much ability I felt she was never very keen.

The Duke of Windsor, now over seventy, has played golf for most of his life. He loves the game and knows all the top players of the world and has played with most of them. Here he is putting, in a cool summer outfit of pre-war days.

The Duke of Norfolk playing the first hole at Cannes. Our premier duke is a fine all-round games player and plays surprisingly well for a casual golfer.

A wartime game in India between Field Marshal Earl Wavell and John Goodman, 1933 U.S. Open Champion, then a private in the U.S. Armed Forces. Despite the fact that our famous soldier had lost the sight of one eye he was a useful player in a game he had loved from boyhood.

Lord Brabazon and I enjoyed a game together at Mougins, Cannes. Lord Brabazon, who died in 1964, at the age of eighty, was one of our greatest all-round sportsmen.

The Earl of Carnarvon puts, croquet fashion, watched by the Earl of Derby. Both men are keen golf fans. Lord Derby, President of the P.G.A., is a keen player with a long drive but he cannot find time to play as often as he would like because of his many commitments.

A blind man playing golf at an American Army hospital. It is not easy for the player or the teacher, but it obviously gives the player great satisfaction to feel he can continue to play the game even without his sight. For putting, a little bell is rung to give the player the idea of where the hole is located, but it is quite a difficult task to get him set at the address to play the shots.

Sir William Carr, one of the leaders of Fleet Street, who is a life-long golfer himself and a member of a big golfing family. Sir William is President of the famous Walton Heath Golf Club, where the News of the World Tournament (now the News of the World P.G.A. Matchplay Championship) was born over sixty years ago. It is the oldest major professional event in the world and almost the only remaining matchplay event. Professionals dislike matchplay; they get defeated quickly and they hate packing up so soon.

World famous pianist Bruno Mosievitch was a keen golfer. He found it kept him fit for his exhausting life as a star pianist with its long hours of essential practice.

Fred Daly, 1947 Open Champion, and Eric Brown,
Scotland's leading professional since the war, surround
Arthur Askey, the little genius of the Music Hall.
Daly has now retired from major golf. Brown still has
flashes of brilliance. A former stoker on the railways,
Eric had to wait five years after turning professional
before he could play in tournaments and win prize
money. This stupid rule has now been rescinded by the
P.G.A., but it was a big handicap to Eric Brown in his
younger days.

Bing Crosby driving. He often plays with a
pipe in his mouth.

My wife and I join the 'My Fair Lady' team, Rex
Harrison and Stanley Holloway, also Mrs. Laney
Holloway, for a game of golf at Sands Point Golf Club
in New York

A round with Bob Hope at St. Moritz. As much a
comedian off the stage as on it, Bob lives for golf. He
never misses a chance to play and 'shoots in the high 80s'.

The late Ian Fleming, creator of James Bond, and a personal friend. In the famous Bond thrillers the hero often plays golf, always using Henry Cotton golf clubs. This was partly because Ian liked the clubs and partly as a personal compliment to me. He once told me that he took his James Bond likeness from a photograph of me he saw in my book This Game of Golf. A very nice compliment indeed!

Two sturdy kings of the restaurant world. In cap Marcel Terrats, of 'La Mere Terrats' on the Cote d'Azur and Henri Sartori, founder of London's famous Coq d'Or Restaurant. With them is Hilaire Giraud, professional at Cannes Country Club.

Golf can be taught individually or in classes, for it is a game that has to be learned. The so-called 'natural' golfers are those lucky enough to have the necessary muscles to swing a golf club fast and accurately; the rest of the world has to build these muscles. This takes time and perseverance, but the satisfaction is great! Here I am sitting among a group of keen Irish golfers during a teaching visit to the green isle.

Anything can happen in golf

Golf is the most fascinating game. Anything can happen in a round of golf . . . and it usually does. Other games have rules which can be summarised in short booklets and which suffice without variation over the years. But golf is vitally alive with an ever-changing personality which constantly produces the most amazing situations, so complex and often so absurd that they could not have been envisaged by even the most farsighted rulemakers. This is why there are so many rules, with additions and riders; and to cover still further eventualities the Royal and Ancient committee have compiled a number of thick volumes filled with answers to conundrums sent in by puzzled golfers.

Someone once wanted to know what he should have done when his ball hit a high branch of a tree and stayed there. Archie Compston could have told him. When Compston's ball did this trick in a tournament at Queen's Park, Bournemouth, Compston climbed the tree, his club clenched in his teeth in the best tradition of a golfing Tarzan. Balancing precariously, he played the ball onto the fairway and near to the green. Arnold Palmer coped with a similar situation in an Australian tournament last year when he dislodged his ball from a tree with his Number One iron.

A golf ball is no respecter of sex either; a lady golfer once found her ball firmly ensconced in a bird's nest. It was an awkward position to cope with, especially in front of a staring crowd. But the match was a tight one and the lady was an enthusiast, so dignity was sacrificed to the game in the only possible solution. She bravely climbed the tree and, having assured herself that there were no eggs or young birds in the nest, she played the shot on to the nearby green and sank the putt to halve the hole.

Golf balls are inveterate travellers. Railways lines frequently run by the fairways, especially in Scotland, and many a frustrated player has watched his ball journey away from him in the open-windowed compartment of a moving train or in a wagon of a passing goods train.

Balls have a propensity for landing in the pockets of spectators and have an uncanny way of not announcing their arrival. Walking down a path near the Hesketh Golf Club one afternoon a clergyman put his hand into his pocket and brought out not his handkerchief but a golf ball. He had no idea when it had arrived nor how it had done so without attracting his attention.

Playing in a Championship at Turnberry, Lady Ellis lifted her ball out of casual water and dropped it over her shoulder. Turning to play it she found that the ball had vanished. It was eventually found in her jumper, where she had apparently dropped it down the loose neckline.

Aubrey Boomer once skied a shot and waited, with mounting impatience, for it to come down. It never did. After a long search he discovered it in the pocket of his jacket.

Golf balls have wanderlust. They have been found hiding in discarded boots, in tins, in handbags. Many are found in birds' nests; some having been misdirected there by players and others carried there by magpies and crows who have quite a predilection for them.

The classic example of the awkward situations in which a ball can place a player is the incident which resulted in Harry Bradshaw losing the 1949 Open Championship. When his second shot to the long 5th hole finished in the bottom of a broken bottle he lost a shot playing the ball from the glass. He took six for that hole; with a five he would have been champion. The rules were later clarified and it transpired that he could in fact have lifted the ball without penalty. But he was not sure and rather than risk disqualification he played the ball from where it lay, in keeping with the standard rules of golf.

I have seen a golf ball with a wooden tee peg sticking far into it. A topped drive had driven the ball into a tee lying in the grass.

Try as we may to form comprehensive rules which envisage every eventuality and to eliminate every element of luck, golf eludes all our efforts to harness and tame it. The very essence of the game is adventure and a great part of its attraction lies, I think, in its resemblance to life, with the player facing unexpected dangers and dealing with unfortunate situations as they arise. It is a challenge impossible to resist.

In Strange Places. The game that has presented its players with strange problems has been staged in many unorthodox settings over the years.

Perth golfers on the North Inch claim that they once kept their clubs on the site of a temple to Mars, while many courses in Britain contain ancient memorials and landmarks of Pictish forts and Druid stones and Celtic churches.

History was enacted alongside the pathways we follow

A Victorian crowd surround the 1st fairway of the Old Course at St. Andrews to watch the local fire engine being put on test. The scene today is different but the buildings in the background, the clubhouse, the old Grand Hotel behind the 18th green and Rusack's Hotel on the right, look the same today as they did nearly one hundred years ago. Rusack's is now the leading hotel in the town. This is scarcely to be wondered at, for there are few hotels in the world with a better location than this old one: right on the eye of the 1st fairway of the most famous golf course of them all.

Weather is no deterrent to the determined golfer. Putting in a gale, this player has turned his cap round to keep it from blowing off. His caddie waits patiently nearby, leaning against the wind.

An unusual golfing memory of 1930 from the Mar del Plata Golf Club in Argentine, where a camel was used to transport sea sand to fill the bunkers. This forty year old camel carried five hundred pounds of sand and often worked all day, making this quite an economic operation.

A pre-war scene at Walton Heath Golf Club, which has the two most famous heathland courses in the world. The course is never wet at any time of the year but after a cloudburst the water cannot escape, even on the driest course. The storm over, the green staff hasten to remove the water so that play can be resumed.

A close-up of the Harry Bradshaw bottle incident which I re-enacted for a television film. This shot was taken during a rehearsal. The camera, of course, just caught the flight of the ball into the bottle, my hand and the stone were out of view.

on our rounds. The second hole of the Pitlochry course in Perthshire runs close by the site of the Old North Road, along which Robert Bruce withdrew his shattered forces after his defeat at Methven, while Moor Park once belonged to Cardinal Wolsey after whose fall it went to the equally ill-fated Duke of Monmouth, whose home has now been turned into the clubhouse.

The story of the development of golf in Europe begins with an engaging story of the Peninsular War. It appears that two Scottish officers, who were billeted at Pau, celebrated the 1814 victory of Wellington at Orthez with a game of golf, having packed clubs in their kit in optimistic anticipation of such an occasion. Twenty years later these same two soldiers returned to Pau on holiday, again taking their clubs with them. Apparently their enthusiasm was infectious, or perhaps the inhabitants of Pau were just catering to the whims of these peculiar Britishers. Either way, Pau was the first of many Continental resorts in which golf was introduced for the pleasure of British holidaymakers.

The Scot who introduced the game into the Pacific Northwest coast of America encountered many difficulties. The first course was a prairie; this he overcame by simply rolling a green on the main fairway to make a three-hole course. But when it came to importing clubs the customs agent had never heard of the game and he was quite at a loss to decide into which official category clubs fitted. At last he reached a decision. 'I'll enter them as garden tools as you will probably be digging up ground anyway.' So the first golf clubs paid duty as implements. A very singular one-hole course at Singapore was situated between the gaol and the hospital. The names of the

Where the sea was the fairway: the driving range for a time on the pigeon shooting terrace at Monte Carlo. Floating balls were hit to anchored dinghies some sixty feet below in the blue waters of the Mediterranean and collected by fishermen in boats who scooped the balls from the water. When live pigeons were brought back shooting was substituted for golf. At the wish of Princess Grace of Monaco clay pigeons are now used instead of the unfortunate live birds: a happy and humane substitution.

A disconsolate rain-soaked crowd trudge home after learning that play had been abandoned for the day during the 1961 Open Championship at Royal Birkdale. The greens were flooded and play cannot continue once the holes are under water; there can be puddles lying on the green but the actual hole must not lie beneath the water level.

holes might well have taken all joy out of the game as they included the Cholera green, the Smallpox green, the Mortuary, the Gallows and the Gaol. I have never been able to verify if the Gallows was, in fact, the final hole. It would be rather a cheerless note to end on!

A dramatic setting for golf was against the barbed-wire fences of British prisoner-of-war camps in Germany during the last war. The equipment was not elaborate: often one club and one ball, skilfully made of old gym shoes, was shared by all the prisoners in the camp. The ball was no less elusive than most golf balls; it displayed scanty respect for restrictions and would often land outside the barbed-wire compound. If the guard was friendly the prisoners were allowed to retrieve the ball.

And so the game goes on, in all circumstances and in all weathers; in war and in peace; among royalty and among ordinary people; for fantastic sums of money and just for the gentlemanly pleasure of winning, or even losing. A pastime has become a sport and a sport an industry, through the power and fascination of a little white ball that girdles the globe.

Golf being played by British prisoners in a camp in Germany during the war. This shows one player passing the only club the camp possessed to his opponent, while the gallery of prisoners follow the game.

St. Andrews is the mecca of golfers all over the world. Just so golfers visiting America must see and play on Pebble Beach on the Pacific coast of California. Here the huge ocean rollers crash against the rocks bordering the holes and seals bark enthustastic support, or criticism, from the rocks jutting out of the water not far from the shore.

This course is open to the public and often major tournaments are held on this testing layout. It can really blow here, and some of the world's best players have returned abnormally high scores on this unusual course.

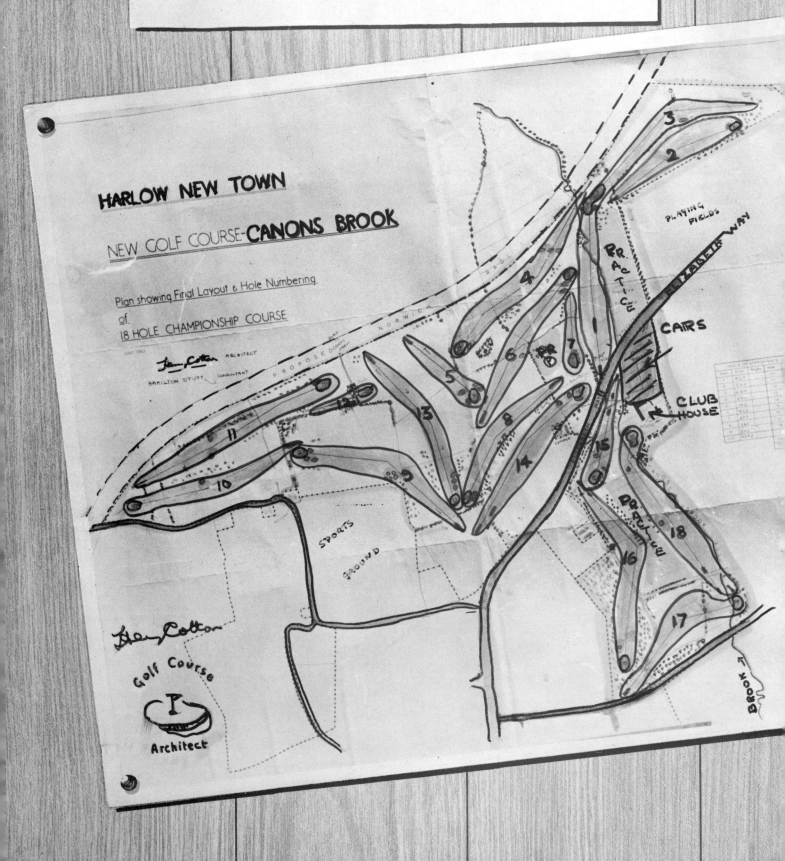

HARLOW NEW TOWN

NEW GOLF COURSE—CANONS BROOK

Plan showing Final Layout & Hole Numbering.

of

18 HOLE CHAMPIONSHIP COURSE

JUNE 1963

Henry Cotton   ARCHITECT

HAMILTON STUTT   CONSULTANT

Henry Cotton

Golf Course

Architect